MAKING ADULT DISCIPLES:

learning and teaching
in the local church

Anton Baumohl

D1612739

Scripture Union
130 City Road, London EC1V 2NJ

© 1984 Anton Baumohl
130 City Road, London EC1V 2NJ

Reprinted April 1986

ISBN 0 86201 291 0

Phototypeset by Wyvern Typesetting Limited, Bristol

Printed in Great Britain at
The Bath Press, Avon

Foreword

There has been a revolution in secular teaching of which the Church, by and large, appears to be unaware. The average preacher does not know the processes through which learning takes place and as a result his ability as a teacher is severely affected. In the majority of churches the sermon is still considered to be the main way of reaching people and little attention is given to such questions as 'how do people learn?' and 'what is the best method of teaching the Christian faith?'

For this reason, therefore, I am excited by Anton Baumohl's book because he makes available to clergy, pastors and lay-people insights and ideas hammered out over many years of experience. And, what is more, the author practises what he preaches. Depth is combined with a lightness of touch, and many practical examples are given as to how the sermon, the talk and other ways of reaching people, may be enriched and enlivened by taking into account the learning process.

I have no doubt that careful reading of this book could lead to fundamental changes in our approach to Christian discipling. Surely, if we regard Christ as the Truth we owe it to him to be as professional and as thorough as possible. In the wake of Mission England Anton Baumohl's book is both timely and significant and it is with the greatest of warmth that I commend it to all those who have been given the task of teaching the People of God.

DR. GEORGE CAREY
PRINCIPAL OF TRINITY COLLEGE, BRISTOL

Acknowledgements

I would like to thank all those who read the early manuscript and offered their reactions and advice, particularly Peter Gifford, Rev. Colin Matthews and Rev. John Wesson.

Thank you to Jill, my wife, Christopher Griffiths and Bev Tidwell for pounding away at the typewriter.

Contents

1 Liberating our learning

ASSUMPTIONS 8
CHANGES IN SOCIETY 9
TEACHING IN THE CHURCH 10

1
Liberating our learning

One obsessive schoolboy longing of mine was to have a maths book with the answers in the back. It became one of those recurrent dreams: I sat glumly in the classroom at the beginning of a new term as the maths text books were handed out, my heart sinking as I looked through the complex brain-teasers in store, until I reached the back to find I'd been given the answer book. The short-cut to success.

However much we were told that the method of finding the answer was as important as the answer itself we still longed for the short-cut. To a large extent the church in the western world has a similar attitude to *discipleship*. There has been great stress on the 'answers' or the nature of discipleship – the beliefs, attitudes, understanding and behaviour of the Christian disciple – but relatively little emphasis on the means by which discipling occurs.

Assumptions

The shelves of Christian bookshops are packed with a multitude of titles on almost every aspect of Christian living. Unfortunately, the same choice of books does not greet the leader who wishes to think more deeply about the process, the 'how', of discipling. Traditionally the 'how' has been achieved through teaching activities like the sermon or study group or by encouraging personal devotions and study. The purpose of this book is to offer a deeper study of the means by which adults can be discipled in and through the local church. It is based on the assumption that the *way* we help adults in their Christian discipleship is important to their growth. I have chosen to call this process *discipling* and the word is used here to refer to the wide range of activities that enable a Christian to grow as a disciple. *Adult* and *adulthood* are two further words requiring definition. For the purpose of this book I regard adults as those who have reached a level of maturity (socially, mentally, emotionally, physically) that enables them to have a significant level of independence and autonomy. In broad terms this is the eighteen-plus age group – there is no upper age limit.

Another assumption underlying these pages is that discipleship involves growth *throughout life*, and that this is the picture painted in the New Testament. Growth may not be at a steady rate, but it does continue right through to death, and includes periods of regression as well as advance.

This growth gradually takes the Christian towards wholeness in body, mind and spirit and in his relationship with God, with others and with God's creation. It enables him to be more the person God wants; to become more like Jesus, the Son of God who came to reveal the nature of true discipleship. For this to happen there must be continuing change, as our understanding of God expands and as we glimpse more of his nature and work. Our attitudes and values alter as we face new challenges in discipleship, and all this becomes evident in our behaviour and actions. Change is not easy, especially for adults. This book is about encouraging that growth and change.

In the West the church has unwittingly absorbed many of society's attitudes and values. In this respect church and society have worked together to create an unbiblical view of adulthood – as a place of arrival which, when achieved, marks the completion of the learning process. In society, full-time education is seen as the *preparation* for adulthood. Once the school has fulfilled its responsibility the new 'adult' is left to sink or swim. In the local church we often restrict the use of the term 'learning' to the activities of the Sunday School or other work amongst children and teenagers. Often there exists a clear distinction between Sunday School and the 'adult congregation', both physically (the fact that they meet in separate places) and in the methods used. Many adult Christians view the children in the church as those being taught and prepared for adulthood. In both cases we end up with a view of adulthood as something to aim for, a goal for our growth, a place of arrival rather than a continuation of the journey.

Changes in society

Society, however, is moving on and at increasing speed. There are changing attitudes to adulthood and a revival of interest in the way adults are educated. Three important reasons for these changing attitudes are:

1. The need for adults to be increasingly flexible in the way they make a living and in the way they live. Science and technology are rapidly altering our work and leisure patterns. No one starting out on a career now can know how relevant their training will be in ten years' time. Many will have to re-train or at least be prepared for continuous updating, or even consider a complete change of career. In ten years' time home computers will be commonplace, altering the way we shop, arrange our finances and organise our time. Our children will think them commonplace but we will have to learn to adapt. Technological change has created an urgent need for ongoing learning throughout life.

2. The spread of unemployment has also created the need for adults to learn new skills and to take on new roles mid-way through life. We may know of people in our own churches who have had to re-train or find new ways of using their time as the result of redundancy.

3. There is an increasing awareness that adulthood is made up of various phases and transitions – periods of natural change – that adults often need help in coping with: the change from school to work, single to married, childless to parent, work to retirement, companionship to bereavement. This need for help is being taken up in adult education and words like 'continuous' and 'life-long' education have entered the vocabulary. The scope of Open University programmes increases, with short courses on preparing for retirement, educating for leisure, and parenting. More and more community-based groups are offering opportunities for adults who wish to go on learning, either to get more out of life or to cope with it more effectively.

The whole field of adult education is a major growth area in society today and the church must not lag behind by neglecting the needs and the growth of the adult Christians who fill its pews. Not least is the need to help Christians cope with the changing world in a way that is compatible with their faith. Adults in the church need to see the importance of continuous learning as a part of their discipleship and the church needs to understand adult learning if it is to encourage change and growth. Unlike 'secular' educational institutions that still struggle to attract adults to classes, the local church is in a unique position with a captive audience of regular attenders. This gives us a tremendous opportunity, and the responsibility, for assisting adults in growth that affects every aspect of their lives. And this is what discipleship is all about.

Teaching in the church

For decades the church has been concerned with the quality of teaching offered to its children. Today, in most churches, Sunday Schools take some account of the way children learn. So children are no longer offered long talks in medieval English. Instead, teachers use visual aids and modern versions of the Bible and children are involved through drama and activity work. It is time to do the same for adults by focusing more attention on how they learn. We know from our experience with children that teaching and learning are two different activities and that the former does not necessarily result in the latter. As this is also true for adults we must begin to pay attention to the quality of learning as well as the quality of teaching.

In comparing adult and child it is important to see that there are both similarities and differences in the way they learn. Like children, adults learn more effectively when they are participating, and active rather than passive methods of teaching are most effective. Adults also find concrete images more readily understandable than abstract ideas. Understanding the personal relevance of any teaching is vital to learning. Unlike children, adults have a store of knowledge and experience which have profound effects on their learning, sometimes forming a good foundation on which to build and at other times creating obstacles to their growth. For adults, learning is rooted more firmly in the present and a great deal of time is spent coping with the issues and problems of living. Adults also provide a broader, more complex range of differences. Because of past experiences, present circumstances, personality and developmental phases, an average group of adults shows more differentiation than a similar sized class of children.

The church must begin to encourage adults to see the link between discipleship, learning, growth and change. It needs to help adults see that discipleship is not just about 'understanding the faith' but about learning how to live it, and that *learning* is concerned with change that will lead to *growth*. We may have to create in our fellowships the expectancy that change will occur. God continues to ask us to change our ideas, actions and attitudes throughout life, and at times he may even ask us to unlearn ideas we have accepted or ways of living we have developed in the past. Adulthood is not a place of arrival but simply represents a *different* period of life where learning and change continue.

The church has an important part to play in helping adults live out their Christian faith in a changing world. One way it can do this is to make adults aware of the variety of ways in which God speaks to his people. Understandably, many Christians believe that God only speaks through the

10

Sunday sermon or times of personal devotion; that learning about God is purely a mental/intellectual process and doesn't involve the emotions; and that learning is an individual activity with no corporate dimension to it. As we help the learner, we as teachers also have to allow our attitudes and understanding to be challenged – evidence of our own willingness to grow as disciples.

It is my hope that this book will be a stimulus to all who teach adults, and will help liberate learning in our churches from the doldrums in which it is often found. This will involve challenging existing attitudes to adulthood, to teaching and learning, and perhaps to the nature of discipleship itself. We will examine the distinctive nature of adulthood with its peculiar needs and problems and consider the methods we use to disciple and the skills we need to teach. Each chapter concludes with one or two practical exercises that can be used as aids to your own reflection on what you have read and on your own experience and understanding.

Exercises

1 List anything from this chapter that touches on your own experience either at the present or in the past. Put an * by any items that you feel you would like to consider more carefully.

2 List the opportunities for learning that exist in your church.

2   Discipling: a biblical perspective

2
Discipling:
a biblical
perspective

The Bible provides important insights into the discipling process as well as explaining the nature of discipleship. Some of these insights are gained by considering the Bible's overall teaching; some is legitimately gained through study of individual lives and specific passages of teaching. In some respects the New Testament provides the richest source of material and certainly has more obvious links with discipling in the twentieth century. The Old Testament, however, also has much to contribute as it records God's attempts to communicate with man, and man's attempt to make sense of these experiences.

Discipleship – process not state

The New Testament, and particularly the Gospels, provide us with both a model and some understanding of the word disciple. Here it refers to a learner or someone who is taught. If we examine the experiences of Jesus's disciples we can see that the 'pupil' was more than just a passive listener; he actually tried to emulate the teacher (Mark 1:17–18). This apprentice image carries with it a sense of growth or development, as well as a state of being. The disciples had a relationship with Jesus that was immediate but they had not achieved all they could in terms of knowledge, understanding, skills and behaviour (Matt. 15:13–20). This suggestion of growth and development is continued into the life of the early church, and the latter half of the New Testament again portrays a Christian disciple as someone who has to mature and progress. Nowhere is there any indication that the disciple reaches a stage where the discipling process stops. The process is evident in the lives of biblical characters as well as in the more abstract teaching that appears in the New Testament.

The importance of life experiences as a source of learning cannot be overstated and is illustrated in numerous incidents. For example, the Jewish nation discovered much about God's character and concern for them through the events of the Exodus (Exod. 12–14). The experiences of forty years of wandering in the wilderness area of Sinai helped to develop that understanding and to mould attitudes (Exod. 16–20; 32–34). David's early experiences as a shepherd proved valuable preparation for his role as fugitive, king and politician; and the traumatic love affair and cover-up (2 Sam. 11) changed him and his future. Job's reflection on his illness and misfortune proved a time of growth for him (Job 1–3).

The three disciples accompanying Jesus during the transfiguration (Mark 9:2–13) came back changed, as did Peter after his denial (Luke 22:54–62) – a lesson which must have proved very hard, as well as leaving an uncomfortable memory. Peter's dream resulted in some fundamental learning about the nature of the gospel (Acts 10:9–23).

Each experience, whether pleasant or traumatic, was a source of new learning. Whether the lesson had a permanent effect on those involved is not always made clear. What is clear is that they were not planned by those on the receiving end to be part of their course of study but, despite this, they were used by God as a means of helping his people grow in some way. These experiences can be contrasted with the more formal teaching prepared by the priests, administered by the prophets, communicated in wise sayings, spoken from the lips of Jesus or written at the hand of one of the apostles. The knowledge of the history of the Israelites which was carefully passed on from generation to generation within the family (Exod. 12:26, 27), and the celebration of the Lord's

Supper and passing on of basic Christian 'doctrine' in the homes of early Christians (1 Cor. 11:23–26; 2 Tim. 1:5; Eph. 6:4), are both examples of more formal teaching that have their counterpart in the life of the Christian church today.

One of the ways people made sense of these experiences was to dwell on them and to re-tell and discuss them (Deut. 6:4–9). The Exodus continues to be to this day an event to be remembered and re-explored (Deut. 8:2–20). David (and others) recorded some of their reflections on life in the form of song or poetry and many of the Psalms provide us with a commentary on the lives of people who were growing, changing and struggling (Ps. 3, Ps. 18). Being God's people or a follower of Jesus is never portrayed in the Bible as a separate dimension to life but is clearly seen as encompassing the whole of life. The Old Testament provides repeated evidence of God's concern for the social, political and economic livelihood of his people (see the laws in Deuteronomy covering social, economic and political aspects of life, Deut. 19–28; also the prophetic warning, Amos 2; 5). Examination of the lives of both Old and New Testament personalities reveals how a relationship with God touches every aspect of an individual's being: physical (particularly in the area of health), emotional and psychological (attitudes and values, responses and decisions, relationships and communication), intellectual and mental (knowledge and understanding), social, spiritual.

In order to educate his people so that their total existence could be influenced and changed God has used a variety of means ranging from formal teaching to daily experiences. At times the changes were traumatic and in this respect God has never been a respecter of age – Abraham had to uproot at the age of seventy-five (Gen. 12:4); Sarah and Elizabeth both had to wait until old age before experiencing motherhood (Gen. 17:15–22; Luke 1:5–25); Paul was a grown man when his allegiance was challenged. For disciples, the process of learning and change appears to be life-long.

Jesus the discipler

If we now turn our attention to Jesus as one who provides a model of a discipler it is interesting to see the insights he had into human needs in terms of learning. His approach to people varied, bearing some relationship to who they were, what they did or the culture in which they lived.

The twelve disciples received the most intense experience of discipleship. In the twelve we see a small band of people growing in their relationships with one another, developing bonds that were to help them through hardship and provide the foundation for the New Testament church. This shared life was part of their discipling process and fitted in with the formal teaching they received and the events they witnessed during their time with Jesus.

Change was, without doubt, an important element of learning to be a disciple. Jesus challenged those outside the kingdom to change but he also expected his disciples to go on learning and changing (Luke 18:18–30). Change for many of the Jews, especially the more educated ones, involved a radical revision of their existing understanding of the Messiah – the uprooting of centuries of teaching. Some found these changes impossible and were unable to throw out past beliefs and experiences (Matt. 12:1–8; John 7:25–36).

Where there was formal teaching Jesus used a variety of methods, often starting from one experience or incident, or using vivid and familiar pictures as in the parables. He also sent his disciples out to practise – learning 'on-the-job' (Luke 9:1–6, 10).

One astounding element of Jesus's approach to discipling was his challenge to the traditional pedagogical approach where it assumed that children were taught by adults whose wealth of knowledge and experience gave them the natural right to assume the role of teacher. On one occasion Jesus placed a child in the middle of the disciples and suggested that the answer to some of their questions might be in the hands of the child (Matt. 18:2–5). This is not just an isolated incident as Jesus's regard for the resources of children is reflected in other comments.

Paul the discipler

Paul's approach to discipling again underlines the importance of growth, change and struggle in being a disciple. To Paul the disciple was someone maturing in Christ, involved in a race or battle (1 Cor. 9:24–27) – images that suggest something continuous rather than a state that is quickly achieved.

Paul, like Jesus, was concerned about the communal dimension to learning, and the establishment of churches provided a context in which the continuous process of discipling could be focused and nurtured. Discipling was not limited to the occasions when the Christian community met – Paul's own growth was in part a result of his experiences, beginning with his meeting with the risen Christ on the road to Damascus (Acts 22:1–21). The church became the place where learning was sharpened up and where people could find support for their growth-struggles. Paul was also a man who reflected on life and its lessons, and both shipwreck and periods in prison gave him plenty of time to make sense of his life (Acts 16:16–40; Acts 27–28; 2 Cor. 11:16–33).

In analysing the content of Paul's letters we sometimes fail to remember that many were written in response to a need that he perceived in a church or in individuals, or a cry for help from some part of a Christian community. Here we have a prime example of discipling through tackling immediate needs. These letters themselves were, without doubt, a means by which individuals and churches grew.

Finally, Paul invited his readers to look on him as a model and to learn from his behaviour (1 Cor. 4:16,17). Jesus is the supreme model for mankind and hence for the disciple, but the modelling of attitudes, values, behaviour, action and beliefs, appears to be a legitimate means by which people are discipled. Needless to say it has its dangers as well.

The Holy Spirit as discipler

The recurring theme of discipleship and suffering, and the need to fight or at least work at being a disciple, is tempered by the reassuring words of Jesus to his disciples just before he died. In John 14:15–31; 15:26–16:15 Jesus outlines the role of the Holy Spirit as discipler, providing us with a supernatural dimension to discipling. As we disciple adults we need to recognise the two dimensions to that process: one involving human agencies – teachers, group leaders, programme designers, communicators, trainers, pastors – and the other focused on the (sometimes mysterious) work of the Spirit. He leads people into and through experiences that are life-changing, helping Christians to make sense of their lives and God's truth and equipping them with the motivation and gifts to live out that truth in new ways. In recent years the Renewal Movement has borne witness to the discipling power of the Holy Spirit as he has directed people, sometimes quite dramatically, into new understanding, skills, action and behaviour.

Exercise
Choose one Gospel (eg. Mark or Luke) and go through it listing the variety of means by which the disciples learnt. Use two columns to record your findings, one headed 'experiences', the other 'formal teaching'.

3 How learning occurs

3
How learning occurs

Defining the word 'learning' may not be as simple as it first seems. It may help to see it in terms of three elements:

Diagram 1:   **The elements of learning**

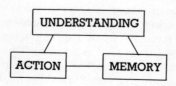

Each of these is important and it is argued here that if any one is missing learning has not taken place.

Mr Smith sits listening to a Sunday sermon during which he hears, for the first time, of the needs of the Third World and its implications for the Christian. Mr Smith *understands* the need and the implications and during the following week various things cause him to *remember* the message of the sermon. When he has been paid at the end of the month he decides to send a donation to a relief fund – he has taken *action*. In this example the learning process is complete. If, on the other hand, Mr Smiths' understanding and memory had functioned effectively but no resulting action followed (either immediately or at some later stage) we might question whether the sermon had really taught Mr Smith anything about Third World needs.

Teaching both inside and outside the church seems to place a lot of emphasis on understanding. This is the goal of much expository preaching, where a major concern is to help people understand what God is saying through the Bible. To a lesser extent there may be a desire to see disciples retain what they have heard or experienced so that it can be of use not only now but in the future. All church teachers would probably also agree that they desire to see action resulting, when those they are teaching apply what they have been taught to their own lives. But often teachers have little knowledge of how to encourage this stage of learning. Action involves applying new information and experience to ourselves, seeing the implications and translating them into the situations in which we find ourselves. The resulting action may be external and visible, exhibited as behaviour; or may be internal, knowledge stored for personal use later, or changes in attitudes or values resulting in a gradual change in behaviour. Teaching methods used in churches often leave the responsibility for application and action in the hands of individuals, without attempting to help them.

Understanding, memory and action are all important in adult learning; and in Christian discipleship we need to take care that our style of teaching does not emphasise one at the expense of the others.

Having defined three major elements of learning you will realise that the process is basically the same for adults as it is for children. Adults may be more sophisticated in many respects, having a greater ability to reflect on and understand their experiences, but the basic process remains the same.

The learning process has been explained in a number of ways and from a number of different perspectives. In order to look at learning in more detail a 'model' has been chosen that provides a broader view of learning than simply 'that which happens when teaching takes place'. It fits more adequately into the picture of God as a teacher who cannot be limited by sermons and instructional methods, but who disciples his people through a variety of formal and informal situations. This model is a tool that will, hopefully, assist those concerned with devising teaching strategies for discipling adults in the local church. But it is an idealised picture and naturally has limitations in its use.

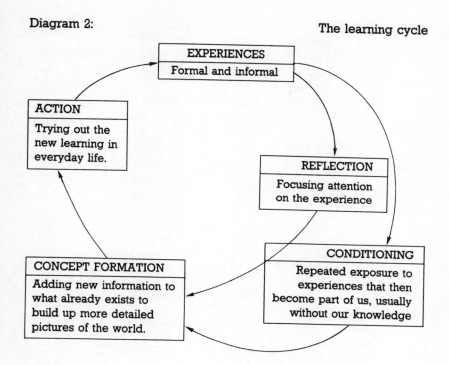

ACTION
Trying out the new learning in everyday life.

EXPERIENCES
Formal and informal

REFLECTION
Focusing attention on the experience

CONDITIONING
Repeated exposure to experiences that then become part of us, usually without our knowledge

CONCEPT FORMATION
Adding new information to what already exists to build up more detailed pictures of the world.

Experience

Any experience or event that we live through during the day has potential for learning. If you think back over today (or yesterday) you will be aware of the vast number of things that you have done or that have happened to you. Many of those events have the potential to bring about change within you – change of ideas, knowledge, attitudes or behaviour. The changes may be small and almost insignificant, or large and life-shattering. For ease of understanding let's divide our experiences into two types, *formal* and *informal*, and illustrate the variety and range through a diagram.

Diagram 3:   Potential sources of learning

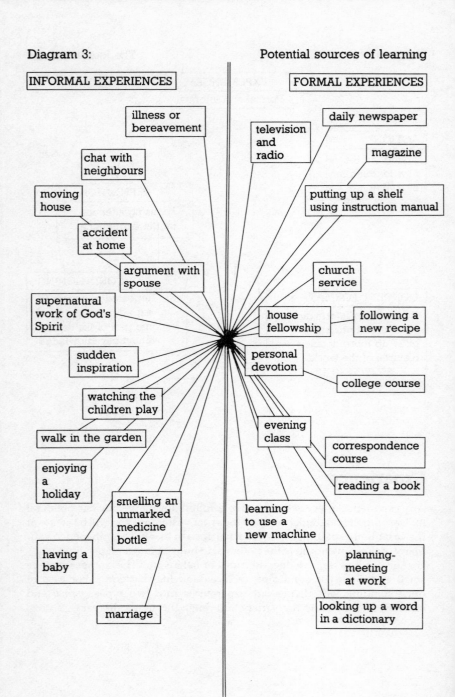

INFORMAL EXPERIENCES

FORMAL EXPERIENCES

illness or bereavement

chat with neighbours

moving house

accident at home

argument with spouse

supernatural work of God's Spirit

sudden inspiration

watching the children play

walk in the garden

enjoying a holiday

smelling an unmarked medicine bottle

having a baby

marriage

television and radio

daily newspaper

magazine

putting up a shelf using instruction manual

church service

house fellowship

following a new recipe

personal devotion

college course

evening class

correspondence course

reading a book

learning to use a new machine

planning-meeting at work

looking up a word in a dictionary

Both types of experience are important in our learning as adults although the experience itself, whether formal or informal, does not necessarily lead to learning. God speaks to us through both types of experience although we often limit our conscious listening to the occasion of formal learning, and fail to hear during the informal experiences. Sometimes the informal experiences can produce the deepest and most long-lasting lessons – a death in the family, an accident, the birth of a first baby, a breathtaking view, a flight in an aeroplane.

At this stage it is important to see that experiences affect us in three ways – physically, intellectually or mentally, and emotionally. Physically we may see, hear, smell, taste and touch the experience. Mentally we are made to think about the experience – we reason and process information consciously or sub-consciously. Finally, experiences affect us emotionally – they provoke feelings of anger, joy, affection, resentment, fear, boredom. The more involved (physically, mentally, emotionally) a person is in an experience the more impact it has. Hence being involved in an accident will be an experience that 'remains with' those involved and may have repercussions well into the future. In church our formal teaching focuses almost entirely on the mind. It is primarily a mental experience and, as such, is limited in its impact. If we wish to make formal learning more effective we need to use as many ways of stimulating learning as we can. A sermon provides learning initially experienced through the ears (physically), the mind (intellectually), and occasionally the emotions (guilt, or excitement, regret, encouragement). The physical side of the experience can be enhanced by using other senses: sight, for example, by the use of visual aids. The emotional side of the sermon experience can be increased by actually asking the listeners to be aware of their emotional reaction to what is being said. Talks and sermons will, by their very nature, be limited in the range of learning experiences they can provide. On the other hand an actual event or incident provides a wide range of stimuli. Life-events often move so fast that the participants do not have the time or awareness necessary to make sense of them in a way that will be helpful later. Adults, therefore, often need help in thinking about and understanding the implications of what has happened.

This picture is complicated by individual tendencies to respond to experiences in one particular way. Some adults are more aware of their feelings and react emotionally; others have a preference for particular physical stimuli such as touch or sight or hearing; others are thinkers. The teaching carried out in most churches assumes that most of us are mentally orientated. This is a false assumption even for the mass of middle-class people that fill church pews, and the assumption needs to be questioned even more rigorously when the adults have their roots in a working-class culture or are non-western.

Those who teach adults need to know how to help adults learn from both formal and informal experiences that use a variety and combination of stimuli, and that have an impact on the emotions as well as the mind. What is vitally important for both teacher and learner to realise is that *both* formal and informal experiences have, for the Christian, a spiritual dimension. Failure to see both types of experience as potential discipling experiences is one reason why so many adults divorce everyday living from their lives at church.

Not every experience, either formal or informal, leads to learning. So much of what happens in a day is lost to us, even to our memories. If we want to ensure that our experiences become part of us we must become aware of them and focus our attention on them. This is the process of *reflection* and forms stage two of the learning cycle.

Reflection

If after watching a television programme we spend time thinking about it we have entered into the second phase of the learning cycle. Reflection may be a conscious act – 'I must sit down and think about this', or sub-conscious, going on in the recesses of our minds. Reflection is part of the mechanism of making sense of an experience. We have already mentioned how Job in the Old Testament spent a lot of time reflecting on his experience in order to make sense of his own life. His efforts paid off and he continued life after his illness and misfortune, a 'richer' man.

Reflection may be a personal, individual activity or may be carried out with others. It is a process encouraged during counselling when the counsellor helps the one being counselled to think about and verbalise what is happening. It occurs in a discussion group when the discussion is the means by which an event, Bible passage or talk are reflected on.

Reflection is an important part of learning but we are not always effective at doing it. More often than not we need help. The process involves thinking about what has happened, remembering events, words, sights and analysing the effect they have had, or are having, physically, emotionally and mentally. Here are some ways of assisting this process:

1 Provide time to reflect, to think, to consider. During a talk or sermon, pause after an important point with an invitation for everyone to digest what has been said and to think about their reaction. Allow silence during a small group discussion before people respond.

(a)   2 Provide a framework for reflection: open-ended questions that will
(b) help people to respond, guidance in how to think about what has been said or what has happened. Encourage an exploration of the experience in terms
(c) of the emotions as well as the mind especially as some people respond more readily through their emotions than with their mind. Questions might include: 'What do you think about that?' and 'How do you react to that?', 'How do you feel about that?'. As teachers we can only guide people in their reflecting, we cannot tell people what to reflect. The outcome of this process

is not in our control and may be different for each individual even though they may have been through the same experience.

Adults need to be helped to reflect on both informal and formal events. They need to be encouraged to think through a sermon on faith and the experience of losing their job or the reason for their faltering answer to a friend's objection to faith. The local Christian fellowship has a vital role to play in providing support in all these instances. The small fellowship group, the close Christian friend, or the Sunday teaching can provide just the opportunity needed. Hopefully, when this happens, we will be producing adult Christians who are more able to integrate their Christianity with their everyday lives.

Conditioning: a short-cut to learning

Within every adult's 'store of learning' there will be items that have been acquired without any conscious effort at all. These result in attitudes and behaviour that are part of us and yet beyond our awareness. Much of this learning has occurred through a process known as conditioning. Conditioning occurs when we are regularly exposed to specific experiences (often informal experiences) until they affect us in some way without our realisation. Some conditioning produces positive behaviour; the infant who is continually reminded when he tries to cross the road without holding mum's hand eventually learns to wait before crossing. A tall man regularly bumping his head on the low ceiling of his new home soon becomes conditioned to lower his head every time he enters. Conditioning can also be negative. Children living in a family where parents continually pour scorn on particular groups in society (because of handicap, colour, social standing etc.) may grow up with a prejudice towards the same group – they have been conditioned.

Adults in the church may be conditioned by what they learnt from the experiences of school days, or their attitude to change may be conditioned by a continual message from society that learning is for children. Those who teach adults in the church may be conditioned to see teaching as simply imparting knowledge – because that is what they, in the past, were exposed to. Individual Christians may believe they are 'no good' when it comes to learning new things because of the negative conditioning they received at home or school. Western Christian males may be conditioned to hide their emotions and not to admit to weaknesses.

Learning that is imparted in this way may be an obstacle to the discipleship of Christian adults. Teachers need to be made aware of their own conditioning in order that they can gently help those they teach to focus on any unhelpful attitudes and behaviour in themselves.

Conceptualisation: becoming part of us

Reflecting on an experience enables the learner to tease out the elements important to him or her – new information, ideas, solutions, understandings, feelings. These are now stored in the mind – what the educationalist would call conceptualisation. We add the new to what is already stored. The brain is a complex storage system and it is thought that similar information or material is stored together or that links are made between similar bits of information. This is the mechanism by which we gradually build up pictures of the things that make up our world. These pictures are called concepts. Throughout our lives our understanding of a particular subject will increase as we add new knowledge and insights to what is already there. Sometimes new experiences reinforce and develop the picture that already exists from past stored material, but at other times they challenge what is there. Many adults find this latter situation particularly difficult to cope with. It can create conflicts which individuals attempt to resolve in one of two ways. They may accept the new and allow it to alter their current picture, perhaps changing it quite radically – this has been called unlearning and may be a painful experience. Alternatively, they may reject the new by ignoring it altogether or rationalising so that it fits what they already understand or believe.

John has never had much time for the church. In the past he has met Christians whose lives he judges to be no better than his. In fact they seem to be hypocrites, believing one thing but practising something different. One day a new Christian neighbour moves in whose life speaks of a peace and kindness that John has not experienced before. It challenges his own ideas. As a result of this experience John may change his attitude to Christians and perhaps to the church. If he does he will be unlearning past beliefs. On the other hand John may reject what he sees by refusing to link his neighbour's action with Christianity or the church, 'He's just a nice chap'.

John provides us with an example of how this part of the learning cycle can proceed from an informal experience. The process is just the same in formal situations such as listening to sermons, watching TV programmes, taking part in discussion groups or reading a book. All these may challenge our picture (understanding) of aspects of discipleship and we can choose to reject or accept them.

Teachers of adults in the church have an important part to play in this phase of learning. Just as teaching schemes may be used in the Sunday School to help children develop their understanding of the Christian faith, so adults can be helped in their discipleship by using a structure. An adult teaching programme can provide a conceptual framework for building new and exciting patterns of living for those involved. It can enable challenging pictures of discipleship to be built up in the lives of adults so that new ideas, information, problems or experiences can be worked at and not put to one side. Teachers need to be aware that they are also building on what already exists in the minds of adults. Do they know where Christians in their church are in their understanding and knowledge? Do they know what their reaction might be to particular issues? We can only discover this by finding time to listen to those we teach and by allowing them to *respond* in some way to the teaching we provide. We do not want new learning to be rejected simply because it challenges old understanding, we want adult disciples to be open to change for the sake of their own growth and maturing in Christ. We need to encourage a climate of what has been called 'critical openness', where new and challenging ideas can be considered in an open way before acceptance or rejection. When we feel the need to present teaching experiences that will challenge old beliefs we have to be prepared for possible responses and provide encouragement and support for any unlearning that might have to take place.

Making it real

In the past adulthood has been associated with the ability to grapple with abstract ideas. Children need picture language but adults can cope with the abstract and do not need to be spoon-fed. This idea must be questioned seriously, as the majority of adults admit to being able to think only in pictures. Informal experiences are generally concrete, they are things that actually occur – are touched, smelt, tasted, seen. They usually remain in the mind as pictures. Those who teach must be able to present ideas in concrete form – an illustration of an abstract idea, a visual aid or picture, an object or even a real experience where learners are actively involved (such as a piece of drama, worship or a simulation exercise). We will be considering this in more detail in chapters five and six.

Practice makes perfect

For many adults the hardest aspect of learning is the application, the last element of the learning cycle. The learner has to translate the experience, whether from a formal or informal situation, into a form that can be put to use. Here we return to the issue of change first raised in chapter one. Whether or not change occurs in the learner depends on what happens at this stage. If the learner makes use of the experience in any one of three ways – 1 by storing information that can be used later, 2 by beginning to develop a new attitude to some aspect of life or establishing new values, 3 by some form of action – then the learning cycle has been completed.

Trainers and instructors in industry have long recognised the importance of helping adults with this phase of their learning. People learning to use a machine are encouraged to practise on the machine as soon as possible after the period of instruction or are trained 'on the job'. Similarly in the church we must not relegate application and action to vague generalities. We need to help adults apply what they are learning about Christian discipleship, not only the facts but feelings and behaviour as well. The Christian who recognises that he gets excessively angry or aggressive or that he withdraws from difficult situations needs to see how to use his new insights to develop more positive responses in the future. The adult who discovers a gift or develops a skill may need help in seeing how it can be used in the different situations in which she finds herself. The disciple who learns something more about who God is, or the significance of Jesus's ministry needs to see how that affects his daily living. One of the reasons why adults find this stage so difficult is their inefficiency in transferring what they have learnt in one situation to another. Again we shall consider this in more depth in the next chapter.

Our teaching can assist learners in a number of ways:

1 by providing concrete examples of how the learning may be used or applied;

2 by counselling or discussion which focuses on the application and use of things learned, in order to encourage learners to see the way ahead for themselves;

3 by providing practical outlets, such as participating in evangelistic outreach after teaching on evangelism, or working in a community-based programme after considering the Bible's call to help the poor. Incidentally, when the *practice* starts the *learning* doesn't stop because the experience may start the cycle off again (experience – reflection – conceptualisation – application).

Everyone's different

The picture of learning we have just sketched is obviously simplified and provides only a general framework. We need to complicate the idealised picture by admitting that everyone is different to some extent in the way they learn. Here are just some of the ways we differ:

1 Speed: some people can absorb new things faster than others.

2 Some people prefer to receive material visually, aurally, or through touch; some respond to stimuli more effectively through their emotions than physically or mentally.

3 Some are analytical and are more able to take complex ideas to pieces in order to understand them.

4 Some people have a good memory, others a poor memory.

5 Many are only able to think in concrete terms, a few understand things that are presented in an abstract way.

6 Some are able to reflect on and make sense of informal experiences with little help, others find it very difficult and need more assistance.

Figure 1:   Adult development

Age range   **Some features**

18–30   Search for social identity, particularly through job/
               career selection. Choice of marriage partner and
               learning to adapt to marriage relationship. Estab-
               lishing first base in the community, managing a
               home. Starting a family and coping with young
               children. Christians often active in leadership roles
               especially where child rearing hasn't started.

30–40   Developing skills and experience to further job/
               career prospects. Stable period of life although
               further house moves may create temporary instabil-
               ity. Discovering more of a role in the local commun-
               ity, greater interest in politics. Much energy in child
               rearing and family life.
               Growing reality of staying single and struggle to
               adjust to this.
               Many too busy for church responsibilities.

40–50   Many reach a plateau as far as work is concerned,
               accepting that they have gone as far as they can go.
               Some may look for career change.
               More effort put into non-work activities and develop-
               ing relationships.
               Physical ageing begins to have effect – greater
               illness.
               Ageing parents may create a strain on a family, but
               children are taking more responsibility in the home.

50–60   Work becomes more of a struggle in an attempt to
               keep up the pace.
               Physical ageing continues to have an effect.
               Changes in social and leisure activities may occur.
               Marked decline in sexual dimension to marriage.

60–70   Retirement and general decline in health.
               Social life changes with death of friends and close
               relations.
               Leisure activities are reduced and are less active.
               Many adjusting to the reality of their own death.
               Feeling of less worth in relation to others.

70–80   Concern for survival with reducing health, finance,
               social contacts. General dependence on others.
               Desire to retreat to the past and to block out the
               present. Coping with institutional life and total loss of
               independence.

7 Sex, age, intelligence, personality, and previous experiences all can have an effect on learning.

Adult development

In recent years a great deal of work has been done to improve our understanding of adulthood. One result of this has been the recognition of a number of developmental phases in the life of adults. In applying the learning cycle to our discipling of adults we need to place alongside it this picture of adulthood. Together they may do much to assist our discipling programmes in the local church.

The local church, in its role of discipler, has a responsibility to those adults who seek its help and support: a responsibility to open up the breadth of learning possibilities; to be a place where intentional learning can be encouraged and where even informal and conditioning experiences can be focused on and fully exploited. Those who are given responsibility to aid adults in their discipleship, whether teacher, preacher, leader or pastor, must get to know the adults with whom they work so that what is done is relevant and can be applied by participants to their daily lives.

Exercises

1 What opportunities exist in your church to enable Christians make more sense of their 'informal' experiences?

2 Think about any important lessons that you have learned as a result of your own informal experiences.

3 Look back over the section headed 'Conceptualisation: becoming part of us'. Now think about your own picture/concept of what *learning* is. Has that concept been challenged or developed by anything you've read here? If so what have you done with any new ideas:

– added them to what you already know to produce a more detailed picture?

– used them to create a new understanding, possibly unlearning old ideas?

– rejected them because they don't fit past experience and understanding?

4 Obstacles to adult growth

4
Obstacles to adult growth

Adult learning – a problem area

We have examined one explanation of adult learning in which change is implicit, but we have also hinted that adults often find change difficult. The time has come for the church (as well as society) to do more to promote openness to learning in adults, and to provide positive encouragement and support so that adults are able to take the 'risks' involved in opening themselves to God. The past has contributed unwittingly to many misconceptions, fears and problems that surround adult learning today. One way to create a more positive atmosphere in which discipling can take place is to help Christians confront any obstacles that may be the cause of retarded growth.

To challenge old ideas, to encourage people to face their fears and their misconceptions, will involve some pain both for individuals and the fellowship as a whole. To avoid these issues because of the fear of losing members of the fellowship means that the old unhelpful attitudes and practices continue and 'change' is reinforced as the bogeyman of the Christian church. This can lead us into becoming closed to God and stunted as Christ's disciples. This chapter focuses on some of the common misconceptions adults have about what learning is or involves, the fears adults experience when learning, and the special problems encountered by adult learners. As we examine each of these three areas in turn, try to picture particular adults in your group or church and their possible reaction to challenging learning situations.

Misconceptions regarding learning

Learning is passive and formal

Mrs Briggs is in her mid-forties. She remembers her school days as times when she sat and listened. Discipline was fairly strict, classrooms were austere and children sat in lines behind desks. She wouldn't distinguish between teaching and learning – they are synonymous in her mind, and both are concerned with taking in information and trying to make sense of it. This picture has been reinforced for Mrs Briggs in her local church where the teaching (and also the learning) is associated with preaching. She remains a passive listener as at school, she accepts, on the whole, what she hears, and hears it sitting in a row with others. She sees this as an opportunity to take in information and doesn't necessarily associate it with the need for action. The wives' fellowship does not represent a serious learning opportunity for Mrs Briggs. It is more a time to meet other women and to relax. The informal learning that occurs through Mrs Briggs' experiences of life are often not recognised by her as times of growth in her Christian discipleship.

People like Mrs Briggs (our churches are full of them) have had the passive/formal nature of teaching and learning reinforced throughout their lives. They find it difficult to accept less structured and more active forms of teaching. They may not know how to make the most of a discussion, a role play, or even a film or book.

We could help people like Mrs Briggs in a number of ways:

1 Use the passive teaching occasions, such as sermons, to state and restate the nature of learning, to explain the value of all activities inside and outside the church as potential learning situations where God might teach something about being a disciple.

2 In sermons and talks use examples and illustrations taken from the lives of real people (like Mrs Briggs) so she sees that the informal experiences of life have something to teach her.

3 Make clear and direct links, during teaching, with the sort of action and change that could occur in Mrs Briggs' life and in the life of the church as a whole, as a direct result of what has been taught and experienced.

4 Provide a variety of teaching experiences within the setting of the local fellowship which will demonstrate that learning takes place in a variety of situations. This should include large groups (whole church) and small groups (home group), structured (sermons) and unstructured (open discussions) settings.

5 Introduce teaching methods that encourage more participation on the part of the learner. Mrs Briggs can be coaxed, very gently, into discussion, role play, simulation games etc.

6 Provide opportunities and active encouragement for Mrs Briggs to think about the informal experiences she has at home, work, in leisure activities, and through her relationships with others and, where appropriate, to learn from these.

Learning is only initiated by experts and people in 'authority'

John sits in the congregation listening to yet another superb sermon. He thinks what a privilege it is to have such a gifted preacher as a minister. The mid-week church meeting is equally rewarding and another opportunity to hear the minister use his gifts and training to bring the Bible alive. But at the Works' Christian fellowship John is extremely frustrated by the Bible studies and discussions. There's no one in that group who can really handle the Bible like his minister and discussions rarely end with any unanimous conclusions.

The authoritative preaching of the word of God has a vital part to play in the growth of the Christian, but what has happened to many adults in the church is that they have come to believe that their learning is completely dependent on teaching that comes from people in authority ('people who know what they are saying', the experts). They may be so severely blinkered that they become deaf and blind to God's Spirit as he prompts them through other means.

John can't see the personal application of the comments made by Jane during the Christian fellowship Bible study because she has only been a Christian for two months, and Steve's stuttering contributions are not worth a second thought. For people like John, less structured teaching situations where discussion is open and everyone has a say is not a legitimate place for learning.

John is genuinely concerned that his Christian life should be based on the truth, but he has wrongly assumed that only those in authority and with training can be relied upon to teach the truth. Those with less experience and knowledge or no training may, he assumes, lead people astray. This reasoning is, I believe, based on two misunderstandings. The first is that *growing* as a disciple is simply about knowing absolute, incontrovertible truths. The second is that God's Spirit only communicates truth through trained experts. Most Christians could probably point to important lessons that they have learned through other people and experiences in the absence of 'experts'.

This over-reliance is made worse when ability, experience and wisdom are confused with status and position. Sometimes those who have something to offer others, because of their experience or gifts given them by God, are ignored because they don't have the status or they hold no identifiable office.

John, his minister, and others like them need to understand that there are resources within each human being that provide a wealth of potential material for the learner. However inarticulate or limited in Christian experience others in the fellowship may be, they may be the means by which John grows in his discipleship; but first he must be prepared to listen to them and to take what they say seriously.

In society and to some extent in the church, this over-reliance on the 'expert' (the doctor whose diagnosis is beyond question, the one-man-band vicar, the school teacher who is a law unto himself) is being challenged. It is unfortunate that individuals and churches focus all their learning and teaching on one or two people in authority when many other resources, in the form of other people, are ignored. It is worth remembering that Jesus took a child and asked the disciples to learn from him or her!

People like John can be helped by:

1 Explaining how discussion groups and open Bible studies work, so that group members see their potential for learning.

2 Training those who lead discussions and Bible studies so that they can lead them in the most effective way, ensuring that personal experience and insights are shared, and curtailing arguments that involve a sharing of ignorance.

3 Encouraging people in groups to listen to their peers properly and to weigh up each contribution thoughtfully.

4 Teaching about the different gifts people have in the church and that each has something to offer in terms of building up the church. In this way healing, interpretation, pastoring, etc. can all be viewed as means of helping people to change and so be involved in the process of discipling.

5 Encouraging people to share their own experiences and growth as a way of helping others in their growth.

6 Rotating leadership of groups so that status and position are played down and authority is given instead to those with valuable experience, knowledge and insights.

Learning is the sole responsibility of the teacher

'What a terrible sermon!' mutter a thousand voices leaving a thousand local congregations on a thousand Sundays.

'I'm not going to that Bible study group again; they never seem to talk about anything that's relevant – if only it was led more efficiently', grumbled the frustrated group member preparing to withdraw quietly.

Many adults place the total responsibility for their learning on to the shoulders of the teacher and preacher, or the teaching programme, Bible study outline, or discussion guide. To some extent this may be justified: the speaker may present his material badly, be obscure or a poor speaker; the guides used may be poorly written and deserving of criticism. But often the criticism is not justified or is only partially justified because the disciples have failed to realise that they themselves take some of the responsibility for their learning.

During a sermon or talk the learners have the freedom to listen or not to listen, to discipline themselves to concentrate or to allow their minds to wander. The listeners also take some responsibility in applying the general themes to their specific lives. If they don't agree with what is being said or fail to understand they are often able to take this up with the speaker afterwards. In small groups the individual is free to contribute and to attempt to steer the group into a more profitable direction. Frustration can be shared with a leader privately and the causes discussed.

At a weekend conference a lady objected: 'I came here to learn . . . Not to work!' saying in effect, 'You're the teacher, Teach!' No teacher can take *full* responsibility for our learning and growth as disciples, we each must take some of that responsibility ourselves – it takes effort from the learner as well as preparation by the teacher.

We can encourage people to take some responsibility for their own learning by:

1 Encouraging them to contribute to the planning of teaching programmes so that their needs can be met in some way.

2 Explaining quite plainly the responsibility they have for their own learning. We often do this at the start of a training course by saying, 'What you take away from today is not just in our hands; you have some responsibility, so make your needs known, question things you don't understand, participate as fully as you can, and try to translate what you experience here to your own situation.'

3 Encouraging people to share their criticisms, and then explore with them why they feel dissatisfied. You may help them to discover deficiencies in their own ability to learn. This process is most productive if it is channelled into evaluation sessions when a house group, training course, special teaching series, or sermon series is examined in order to improve its effectiveness and relevance in the future.

Learning is a serious matter

I recently had a letter from a naval officer who attended a training course I was involved in. 'Thank you for reminding me that learning can be fun', he wrote. Many adults see learning as only occurring in a serious, intense atmosphere. It's a pity that the Bible has no record of Jesus laughing, because some adults require that sort of permission before they are willing to relax or enjoy their learning. Despite this absence it seems unbelievable that the God of joy should frown on laughter and fun. During the training course mentioned above, we explored some issues through games, watched video playbacks of people on the course working, shared ideas, and tried out methods in groups. There had been serious times, but we had also generated a lot of laughter and some activities had been carried out in a very relaxed, fun-filled atmosphere.

To some, the odd joke from the pulpit is enough, and parts of our training course might have seemed offensive especially as it was a means of learning about our faith. But we did learn. We need to be sensitive to those adults who see laughter and fun as frivolous, but equally we need to restore to adults the fun of learning. Laughter is an important means of helping people to relax and of diminishing some of the fears brought to the sessions.

We can help by:

1 Using teaching methods that *involve* people rather than allowing them to remain passive listeners.

2 Using ice-breakers and other fun exercises that may prompt laughter and yet have a serious side as well. It is often better to describe these as 'exercises' rather than 'games' in order to suggest an element of work!

3 Encouraging a relaxed atmosphere in learning situations where people feel comfortable and are able to smile at their mistakes. This can be achieved by choosing an informal meeting place, starting the session with coffee or even a meal, and being relaxed yourself as the teacher or leader.

During childhood, games form a very important part of a young child's education. Adulthood is not so different from childhood that it requires us to learn only in a cold and sober atmosphere.

Learning is all in the mind

Susan Rees left school at sixteen; she hated most of it and the list of subjects she didn't get on with was quite extensive. If it hadn't been for domestic science and games, school would have been a total disaster. At thirty-two and a member of a local church, Susan finds listening to sermons very hard, and feels unable to contribute much in her home group discussions (it's hard competing with two university students, a teacher and a high-powered secretary!). She finds it difficult putting what she wants to say into words.

Many of us see learning as an intellectual exercise, something that simply involves the mind through the channel of words. Very few people are able to grasp abstract ideas with ease. Whether we enjoy discussion and argument or prefer action, whether we relish the mental exercise of weighing up a sermon or a discussion or find it hard work, we all need to understand that learning is more than mental exercise. As we see, hear, smell, touch or taste, our emotions may be touched as well as our minds. People like Susan may be more able to identify her feelings than her thoughts. She may be aware of the peace she feels as she takes communion, the burning anger when she hears about injustice, the frustration when she can't express her disagreement in the Bible study group. Learning for Susan involves having the opportunity to become aware of, and to express, her feelings.

It is not just the less academically minded people like Susan who need to be able to express the emotional dimension to their learning. Christians in general often suppress their feelings because they have the mistaken idea that emotions are wrong. Some may have been taught that emotions are dangerous in matters of faith and may be careful not to focus on them. However, human beings were created with emotions and they form a very strong force in shaping our behaviour – our emotions are as much a stimulus to change as are our thoughts. So instead of trying to ignore them we need to be aware of them and be prepared to examine the way they affect us as people – as disciples – both positively and negatively.

There are also Christians who do not know how to express their emotions in front of others – they feel embarrassed showing joy, happiness, tears, anger, uncertainty. This may be more true of men than women although we must be wary of stereotyping the sexes.

Both the teacher and the learner may need to understand more of the emotional dimensions to learning. The teacher needs to know how to involve the learner's emotions in a positive way. The learner needs to know how to identify and communicate his feelings in a helpful way as a result of both formal and informal experiences.

We can help:

1 By encouraging learners to talk about how they feel as well as how they think, in discussion groups, counselling sessions, in training courses, and 'Christian basics' courses. A discussion group leader may say: 'You've shared your thoughts, but how do you feel about this topic – does it frustrate you, excite you, frighten you, or what?'

2 By using concrete examples taken from the lives and experiences of others. The listeners can then identify with people like themselves – and see how emotions have affected their lives and their growth.

3 By sharing our *own* emotions, as well as thoughts, as we teach. This will involve us in taking the risk of being honest especially when our feelings don't quite match the ideals people have of the Christian disciple or of us personally.

4 By helping teachers and group leaders to cope with other people's emotions when they are experienced in a group.

Learning does not involve conflict

I was sitting in a discussion group in which eight adults were discussing a passage from one of the Gospels. The topic under consideration concerned the meaning of forgiveness. One person contributed their thoughts and then a second came in quite strongly, 'I'm sorry but I have to disagree . . .' and there followed an explanation. The discussion continued for a short time but there was obviously discomfort in the group and eventually the discussion petered out and was followed by a period of embarrassed silence. The situation was finally 'rescued' by the leader who relieved the tension by asking another question.

Conflicting ideas and values in any group can create tension, but in many Christian groups often produce exceptionally high levels of anxiety and discomfort. This may be due, in part, to a feeling that this sort of disagreement shouldn't really exist amongst Christians. When disagreements and conflicts do occur we don't know how to manage them, and avoidance or retreat becomes the least painful way out.

Discipleship involves struggle, testing things out, discovering different ways of applying our faith to our often very ordinary lives. It involves success and failure. The differences in our experience, personality, understanding and daily living will lead us to view things differently from other Christians, whether it be the meaning of Paul's teaching on holiness or the way Christians bring up their children. Resultant disagreement and conflict may be submerged under the surface or openly explored. The arena for exploring conflict could be an informal discussion between two Christian friends, a church committee meeting, a training programme, or a house group or discussion group.

Sometimes conflict is internal, inside an individual who cannot decide between opposing views, values, teaching, emotions or experiences. It is often the function of the counsellor or a member of the pastoral team to help a person explore and resolve these conflicts. Conflict can be creative if explored in the right way and, if we are prepared to explore our differences quite openly, we may discover some new understanding of God's will for us.

We can help Christians use conflict creatively by:

1 Producing opportunities for open-ended discussion, where the end product is not already decided by the leader.
2 Teaching the positive value of conflict, and showing the way Jesus used situations of conflict to point out a positive response.
3 Training leaders of small groups and committee chairmen to manage conflict in a positive way, when it arises, so that they feel comfortable encouraging the 'parties' to explore their differences openly and to make decisions based on this exploration.
4 Developing and encouraging pastoral systems that enable people with personal conflicts to find help in exploring and resolving them.

Learning is an individual and private affair
As I listen to sermons on Paul's letters to the churches, I am interested to see how many times the preacher applies Paul's teachings to the individual

Christian rather than to the whole fellowship. But Paul was concerned for the change and growth of the whole group as much as of the individual. The focus of much of our teaching in the local church is on the individual. We rarely hear about what God is saying to us *as a group*, but frequently about what God is saying to *me* as an individual. Throughout God's dealings with man we see him communicating to both individuals and groups – nations, tribes, households, church fellowships. God seeks change both in individuals and groups. The corporate element to learning may be hard for the individualistic, western Christian to appreciate and it can only begin to occur when groups of whatever size are developing relationships that bring people close together. Where there is loving unity in a group, and therefore a willingness to be open to change, they are able to ask questions like:

'What is God saying to us as a whole?'

'How does God want us to grow and change as a Body?'

When this happens learning becomes less private and more public. In this open climate, individuals may be more prepared to share even the hard lessons God is teaching them as individuals. It then becomes possible for others in the fellowship to provide support and encouragement especially where the changes are painful. As adults we need support from other Christians as we learn that growth means change and as we take the 'risk' of making these changes.

We can help:

1 In home groups or church discussion groups by wording some questions in this way:
'What are the implications of this passage/experience/situation/ teaching to us as a group or fellowship?'

2 By encouraging practical support and prayer for people who are taking the risk of being open about the learning in their lives. This may mean training group leaders to be pastors, or having a good pastoral care system that people feel happy to use.

3 By taking the initiative in being open ourselves so that others see our willingness to take risks and to share in common learning in a group.

Fears – real and imagined

Fear and anxiety can be positive emotions in helping us avoid danger or propelling us into some more wholesome activity. They can actually aid our learning. On the other hand they can result in paralysis – mental and emotional as well as physical – causing people to retreat and reject. They can create defensiveness and closed minds and be an impenetrable block to learning and growth in the Christian life.

Those who teach adults need to find some balance – encouraging disciples to face stressful situations when they are necessary but minimising stress when it's unnecessary. Adults have a number of fears in relation to learning.

Fear of ignorance and failure

A number of times I have sat in meetings where the speaker has thrown out questions, not in a rhetorical way, but actually expecting answers. I hate these meetings, and even more so when the speaker seeks the answer by looking (or pointing) directly at individuals. I have this fear of being shown up – of not having the answer or of getting the answer wrong, and I believe it is a fear I share with many other adults. When I go to a meeting where I sense the speaker might get too direct I seek the security of the back row or the centre of the audience hoping for anonymity in the crowd. For many adults, this fear of ignorance or failure acts as a deterrent to their contribution to discussions, willingness to answer questions, give opinions or share experiences. Anxiety may reach its peak in the small group where it is not very easy to hide away. In our fellowships we sometimes create the impression that we *ought* to know the answers (because we are adults). This results in a lot of pretence, and rather than admit our ignorance or uncertainty we bluff our way through.

We can help by:

1 Creating the climate in small groups where people realise that they aren't judged by the rightness or wrongness of their answers. This relies on the skill of the leader and other group members who are able to listen to, and value, every contribution made.

2 Spending time building up relationships between people in groups so that they feel comfortable and able to say what they think or feel. Some of the techniques in chapter five encourage sharing in less threatening ways and can help this process along.

3 Being open about our own ignorance and the incompleteness of our own understanding, so that even those in leadership positions are seen as learners who fail, and who struggle for understanding.

4 Giving positive reinforcement, on the occasions when they *do* open up, to people who are particularly shy and reticent.

Fear of embarrassment

Peter is a respected member of his church; he has a position of responsibility and people come to him for advice. But he is unaware of his own real concern about how other people see him. Above all he wants to be accepted and taken seriously. Peter steers clear of any activity in the church that he's not sure of and opposes doing things in a new way. He is afraid that he may be shown up or embarrassed in any unfamiliar activity. This fear of embarrassment can be rooted in any number of inner emotions – personal pride, fear of ignorance, inferiority complex etc. It can mean that an adult who is used to being seen in one particular role in a church or group, with established ways of behaving and responding, is unwilling to volunteer to take part in more 'outlandish' activities such as a role play or a simulation exercise. They are afraid of losing respect through being undignified.

Embarrassment may also 'paralyse' the shy, retiring Christian, the person who feels unable to put an argument in a clear, logical way, or those with some physical or mental handicap. As we encourage a new attitude to learning and discipleship in the church we are going to be faced with many adults who resist because it requires more involvement on the part of each individual, resulting in more exposure and more chance of embarrassment.

We can help by:

1 Taking risks of being embarrassed ourselves – participating ourselves in the things we want others to participate in.
2 Providing a secure relaxed atmosphere where others can take risks, get involved, and make mistakes.
3 Using new methods gently and sensitively, giving people the opportunity to opt out and watch if they really can't participate.
4 Providing support and encouragement when others in the group take a risk or 'experiment'.

Fear of unlearning and change
'Huh! All these changes – it's just giving in to gimmicks.'

There is a natural tendency in all of us to resist change and the older we get the less happy we are with change. Change creates stress and stress, as we are all aware, is a major cause of illness. To suggest that change is a part of discipleship and closely tied up with learning can create anxiety which some adults may decide to avoid. We may have come across those who have left their local church because they are not prepared to accept (or unable to adapt to) changes taking place. Adulthood as a period of stability goes hand in hand with the idea of adulthood as a place of arrival. Alvin Toffler in his book *Future Shock* considers the problems adults have of coping with the increasing speed of change in the modern world.

We've already considered the essential link between change and discipleship and the need for Christians individually as well as corporately to change in order to remain effective in a constantly changing society. There is, however, a real danger that change can simply become a matter of taking on the latest gimmick. But change must not be avoided because of the potential dangers; it is an essential ingredient of growth and we have to help adults of all ages to face it and cope with it.

A fear linked with change is that of 'unlearning', or being forced to question and reject things we have learnt in the past. There are adults who still cling to Sunday School pictures of some aspects of their Christian faith because they have not been prepared to unlearn partial truths. On occasions resistance to unlearning is linked to an uncertain faith and amongst the most dogmatic defenders of personal beliefs are those who feel unable to cope with past teaching being challenged.

We can help people with these fears by:

1 Being sensitive to what change and unlearning does to groups and to individuals in fellowships, to empathise with how people may be feeling.

2 Deliberately focusing on change in order to help people see it as natural and necessary. Where possible, allowing people to express their fears and anxieties. This is best tackled in smaller groups.

3 Challenging adults when appropriate with the need to alter their understanding/knowledge/attitudes/behaviour.

4 Providing a secure climate for change and unlearning, with pastoral back-up for those who find it traumatic.

Fear of pain

Discipleship as demonstrated by Jesus involved suffering and pain. The disciple is pictured as a foreigner in a strange land, a soldier involved in a battle, a sufferer at the hand of external forces, a traveller on a difficult and dangerous road. Adults may experience pain because of some past situation or because of present difficulties. We all fear pain and for some that fear may be such that they anaesthetise themselves against particular situations or, alternatively, activate a personal filtering system that removes all the painful elements of learning and growth. Teachers who avoid pain themselves, may collude with learners by avoiding things they know may be uncomfortable or painful. Preachers may avoid certain topics in their sermons or group leaders may refrain from using certain types of teaching methods because they encourage participation or promote honest sharing. It is unhelpful to focus too much attention on painful areas but pain should not be avoided.

We can help by:

1 Being aware of the things that cause pain in ourselves and the way we avoid them or cope with them.

2 Being aware of the things that cause pain in others and being particularly sensitive to those we are teaching.

3 Teaching about the nature of pain and suffering in discipleship – through sermon or group discussion.

4 Training group leaders to cope with pain when expressed by others. This may mean giving people time to explain their feelings and reactions, then moving on and returning to the painful subject at a more appropriate time. It may also necessitate, at times, confronting people who avoid painful topics.

5 Developing pastoral systems with people trained to help others cope with painful experiences. This can be through counsellors or pastoral team members or through a home group network.

Fear of intimacy and emotion

Many of the fears we have considered to date are intensified for some adults when they attend a small group such as the house group. Here they are more likely to be exposed to a type of learning that demands their participation. They are unable to hide and become passive listeners. We should add to this the fear that some adults have of the intimacy of close relationships and of exposing their own feelings to other people. Because of these fears people often shun house groups, or twitch nervously when the person leading suggests getting into smaller groups. Despite this the small group remains one of the most effective units for learning which results in growth and change. It is the one structure where a secure atmosphere for growth can be developed and where learning can be encouraged at an individual level. There is probably little we can do for those who are totally incapable of facing the intimacy of small groups, except ensure some form of pastoral link with an understanding individual or family in the church.

We can, however, help the many adults who are members of groups to 'grow into' their groups; in other words, to gently encourage growth into intimacy. Even in groups where the focus is on Bible study and discussion the learning will be more effective if time is spent in helping people to develop friendships. This could come through enjoying meals together, arranging social activities or using ice-breaker exercises. Friendships grow in intimacy so helping people feel free to share emotionally.

We can help by:

1 Developing small groups where quality friendships can be built and people can feel free to be open.
2 Teaching about the nature of fellowship in terms of intimacy for the purpose of sharing and caring.
3 Modelling openness and honesty in the groups we are in so that others can see their value.
4 Using appropriate questions and activities that encourage people to put their feelings into words and by making it known that tears or laughter are acceptable.

Problems associated with adult learning

Finally let us briefly consider seven further difficulties that confront the adult learner: motivation, guilt and failure, past experiences, individual differences, concentration, translation and application, ageing.

Motivation

In some fellowships there may not appear to be any problems in motivating adults. Announce a meeting and a high percentage will turn up; ask for volunteers and the job is as good as done; seek support and it is given. This experience, however, is not universal and generally the more demanding and 'risky' the job or the subject under discussion, the harder it is to motivate people. If adults are to be challenged to continually listen, apply and take action we must expect the effort involved to 'demotivate' many. The comfort of inertia makes the demands of change look unattractive. Although it may be difficult in some situations to get adults to teaching events, it is even harder to motivate adults to commit themselves to a continuous discipling process in their lives.

There are no easy solutions to this barrier but here are some guidelines that may help:

1 Seeing the personal relevance Adults are more easily motivated when they see the personal relevance of what they are doing or learning. If they feel their own pressing needs are to be considered, or that they will receive help in a specific area of their lives, they are more likely to show an interest. We can help this along by focusing some of the discipling on concerns that they have. One example of this is the church that ran a four-week course on 'Coping with adolescents' for the large number of parents in its congregation with teenage children, and resulted directly from one of the deacons picking up moans from parents about their children. The course was well attended and appreciated.

2 Being involved in planning Adults are motivated if they have had some say in the planning, running, or content of a teaching session. 'Let me know what topics you would like to be included in the discussion groups that start after the Summer', offered the minister of a medium-sized city-centre church. After the seven or eight suggestions put forward had been considered alongside other items that the minister wanted to cover, a letter was passed round saying: 'Next session, groups will focus on the following topics – you will see I've tried to incorporate as many of your suggestions as possible into the programme. . .'

3 Variety There is nothing more likely to kill interest than always tackling things in the same way so that people can not only predict what is going to happen but what is going to be said as well.

4 Excitement Excitement and high expectations can be encouraged by lively publicity to advertise a training event, special meeting or teaching project. This may include eye-catching wall posters or an imaginatively worded notice. Excitement is infectious and if those organising an event can communicate their own excitement and high expectations, others may come to see it as more than just another meeting. Many house groups, training sessions, sermons and talks fail to carry any sense of excitement.

5 Making realistic demands Realistic demands help to motivate. Sometimes we demand too much of people and when adults feel they can't achieve what is demanded of them they often, mentally at least, 'throw in the towel'. People need time to learn but sometimes the time demands on Christians are unrealistic. In some fellowships people may be expected to turn out to meetings one, two, or three evenings a week as well as Sunday. Ask yourself the following: 'Do we expect too much of people, should we cut down on meetings?' 'If this new course is necessary what can be dropped or what can people be excused from?' Sometimes it's the content that's too demanding. Too much is packed into the missionary meeting, too much covered by the sermon, too many areas explored in the discussion, too complicated a teaching game used in a short evening. The content needs to be planned so that it can be coped with by the average adult in the time available.

Unrealistic goals or objectives are great 'demotivators'. A training session for new members of the pastoral team cannot provide all the necessary skills for crisis counselling; an evening on understanding the Bible for new Christians will not equip them adequately to cope with the Bible without the use of other aids. As soon as the learner realises that he can't possibly achieve what is being demanded he may well give up. Programmes can be paced so that those attending can cope. This will require sensitivity on the part of the leader who needs to be aware of how people are handling their learning. It requires flexibility on the part of the programme so that sections can be left out if necessary, left over to next week, or new items added. The learners themselves may even play a part in pacing the programme by being encouraged to speak out when things are too fast, too slow, too full, or too ambitious.

6 Being, and feeling, valued People who feel they are valued are more highly motivated than those who do not. This fact was discovered in research done amongst youth leaders which focused on their commitment to the work, their desire to develop their skills and their concern for the needs of the young people. If we want to be motivators of adult learners we need to show them that they are valued, that their contribution in a discussion is valued, that their presence at a course, conference or group is valued, that their role in the church is valued, and that their growth and development as a disciple is valued. Amongst the simplest means of encouragement are the words 'Thank you'. The more words of encouragement and appreciation we can give to individuals the more motivated they are likely to become.

Guilt and failure

I sat listening to a sermon on personal evangelism and as it progressed I sunk lower and lower into my pew with my feelings of guilt and failure. I realised how much I'd tried in the past to share what I believed, how high my resolve had been and yet how many times I'd chickened out. Guilt and a sense of failure are common emotions in teaching/learning sessions. Guilt occurs when we feel we are not living up to values, beliefs or moral standards, and a sense of failure is experienced when we never quite make it, however hard we try.

Guilt is not a totally destructive feeling. In fact, it can be a means of motivating someone to action – and can actually promote learning and discipleship. Failure can be an experience that throws people back on God, so making it possible to find a new way of tackling a problem.

There are times, however, when guilt and failure can hinder growth. Some adults, because of their personality, are more prone to these feelings than others. Guilt can act as an obstacle to growth when the response to it is one of either running away (ceasing to listen, cutting-off or even making excuses) or sliding into depression and despair.

We cannot prevent people from feeling guilty or from failing and it would be a very ineffective form of discipling that tried to avoid creating these responses, but we can help people to cope with their feelings and hence prevent them from becoming blocks to growth:

1 Being open As preachers, teachers, leaders or enablers we can admit to our own experience of these feelings, so that others can see it is possible to live constructively with them.

2 Being sensitive We can be sensitive to those who attend groups that we teach or lead, being aware that feelings of guilt may result from particular issues explored. We can then bring this into the open by explaining that some may be feeling this way and encouraging them to work at positive ways of resolving their failure and guilt (not simply training them to accept it).

3 Training others We can train pastoral leaders to know how to handle those with guilt feelings so that they are able to encourage individuals to talk about their feelings, to explore the cause and to work out actions or develop strategies that will lead them to finding forgiveness and peace.

Past experiences

Past experiences of all shapes and sizes have lasting effects on us all – influencing the way we act in the present and the decisions we will make in the future. Some of these experiences may have a positive effect on us, leading us into growth and maturity. Other experiences may cause retardation in growth and may create personality defects that lead to unhelpful behaviour and decisions. Adults build on the past as they live and learn and grow as disciples – past teaching, past relationships, past encounters with God, past events, past traumas, past joys – past experiences of all kinds. The experiences of school and church and the expectations that they create in adults regarding the nature of teaching and learning have been alluded to in an earlier chapter. Our approach to adult teaching and learning in the church today is based on past experience and the resulting attitudes created. We may have experienced learning as a formal, passive activity and we perpetuate what we have experienced. Here it is sufficient to say that we need to both directly challenge and greatly encourage people if we are to move them on from the past. Sometimes the past produces blocks, which we may or may not be aware of, preventing us from accepting or understanding today's lesson. Sometimes past experiences have conditioned us into behaving in particular ways that may be unhelpful to our discipleship now.

It is important that we realise that *both* teacher *and* learner has been influenced by his own past.

Individual differences

Our traditional, monochrome approach to teaching seems to assume that adults are alike in the way they learn, but as we have already seen in chapter two there are important differences between adults. The church needs to provide a variety of learning opportunities and methods so that, for instance, those who learn more effectively in small groups where there is support and encouragement can be part of a small group, those who are less verbal have the chance to express themselves in other ways (see chapter five), and those who are motivated to learn on their own are made aware of resources available to them.

Concentration

We are all too aware of a child's inability to concentrate and the ease with which they can 'turn off'! *They* usually show it quite clearly. What we often fail to realise is that adults also have limited concentration spans that will vary from individual to individual. The difference between children and adults is that adults do not show their lack of concentration in such obvious ways. Concentration is determined to some extent by the interest created by a particular experience. Some are very easily distracted from concentrating and may lose the thread of a talk simply because someone near them sneezed. Others may find it impossible to concentrate when they have something else on their minds. Helping adults to concentrate should be as much a concern of the adult educator as it is of the Sunday School teacher working hard to keep the child's attention. One remedy that works with all ages is to increase the amount of participation demanded of the learner, a topic taken up in the next chapter.

Translation and application

Some years ago a vicar came to a training course I was conducting for his church's home group leaders. He sat through the course, was extremely supportive, and showed a willingness to take risks in learning himself – a fact which obviously encouraged the house group leaders present. At the end of the course he came to me and told me how he had used some of the methods employed on the course as a management trainer – his job before entering the ministry. He had never seen that the skills he had learnt in management training could be applied in his church situation. He had all the knowledge and skills necessary to be able to train his own house group leaders without calling on someone from outside.

Adults, in general, find it hard to translate knowledge and skills from one situation to another and need more help than we often imagine. Sometimes our teaching leaves adults with an immense jump to make from the 'classroom' to their reality. Those who teach or lead can help by centring talks, discussions and other learning activities in the real world, using illustrations taken from the world of the learners themselves. Application can be even more specific in the form of suggestions given by the teacher or by the learners themselves.

Ageing problems
Traditionally adulthood has been seen as a time when the learning process slows down. Failing memory, lack of concentration and problems of adapting to change, have all been used as evidence to suggest that as we age we are less able to learn. It may be that this state has been partially induced by society itself and recent findings suggest that our minds are able to cope with learning and change further into old age than we once thought. The church could work together with society to open even the elderly to new horizons. The church's concern is with the 'new horizons' of discipleship with Jesus Christ.

Ageing may not necessarily have an adverse effect on an adult's ability to learn, but the physical results of ageing may themselves create problems. Physical discomfort from hard seats, or inadequate heating, poor hearing and failing eyesight can make learning a trial and may so distract that the participant, however actively involved, is prevented from benefiting from the event. This has implications for the design of the physical environment in which discipling takes place (heating, seating, lighting and amplification) or the choice of venue for particular types of teaching sessions. It also requires sensitivity on the part of leaders and teachers who, being aware of those present in their group, may need to speak up, slow down, reduce the amount of movement for some particular exercise, and create the atmosphere where people feel free to say 'Speak up, I can't hear you!'

Wow! what a mass of obstacles! Is it worth going on when there is so much in the way? Obstacles are things to be aware of, and need tackling when they begin to hinder. The aim of this chapter has been to make us aware of the potential hazards as we develop our discipling of adults, so that when we are confronted by them we are not taken by surprise.

Exercises
1 Which of the misconceptions of the nature of learning is ingrained in your own thinking *or* is implicit in the teaching in your local church?

2 Can you identify in yourself fears related to learning as detailed in the pages of this chapter?

3 Using the topics covered in this chapter make a list of three problem areas that are obstacles to discipling in your church and consider practical ways of removing them.

5 Teaching adult disciples: the means to an end

5
Teaching adult disciples: the means to an end

In looking at positive steps to assist adults in their learning we must now turn to the teaching techniques or methods that can help to promote the quality of learning described in chapter three. The word technique (or method) refers to the framework used to order, explore or present the material to be learnt. The sermon is a technique that enables the proclamation of God's truth. Discussion is a method of exploring issues important for the Christian disciple. In this chapter we will focus on a variety of different techniques, some of which may be unfamiliar to you. Try to look at each with an open mind, and think where they might fit the existing teaching structures used in your church.

Methods can be classified according to the level of structure or control provided by the teacher and according to the amount of active involvement demanded of the learner. The method may be structured (asking questions, symbolism) or unstructured (open discussion, silence); passive (audio-visuals, analogies) or more active (role play, experiential exercises). The selection of appropriate techniques is considered in chapter nine.

Proclamation through a talk or sermon remains an important means of discipling adults. It is important to realise that these are both passive techniques, highly structured and usually with an intellectual emphasis. Although this chapter does not focus on the technique of preparing or delivering a talk it does explore methods which, if incorporated, will add a new dimension to their learning value. The use of analogy, symbolism, guided meditation and even silence will help listeners to take more of an active and personal part in the experience.

The second part of this chapter attempts, very briefly, to link techniques with the stages of learning and the problems associated with adult learning. This involves some overlap but should enable the reader to approach the topic from two directions.

A. The methods

It may be important for some to know that all the techniques described here have been used with adults in various situations. It will be of little surprise to say that individual adults respond in different ways to different techniques, some finding them strange at first but seeing the value later, others accepting them right from the start, and a few openly hostile. On the whole, the result of using these techniques to help adults in their growth has been overwhelmingly positive.

Often, when using new or strange methods, we need to persevere. It is important to prepare well, anticipate possible reactions, explain fully what is going to happen and why, and then carry the exercise through attempting to learn from the experience so that things can be improved the next time.

Asking Questions

There are many occasions when we want to ask questions – to check that people understand, to stimulate sharing and discussion, to solve problems, to encourage participation. The art of asking questions is found in phrasing the question to get what you want. The diagram below illustrates four categories of questions.

Diagram 4:   Four categories of questions

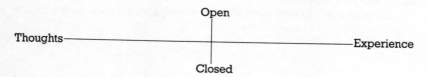

Open

Thoughts ———————————————————|——————————————— Experience

Closed

1 Open questions encourage people to provide a variety of answers and stimulate greater thought and creativity. They are more likely to stimulate discussion, eg.

'What do you think is important here?'

'How would you tackle the problem?'

2 Closed questions encourage a limited range of answers and might be used to get information or opinion on a factual question, eg.

'Do you agree?'

3 Thought-based questions encourage people to respond with their minds and are the most frequently used in Bible study groups, eg.

'What did he say?'

'Why was that happening?'

4 Experience-based questions encourage people to respond from their emotions, eg.

'How did you feel when she said that?'

Here are some examples of the four categories of question:–

1. Open/Thought: 'What do you think the weather will be like tomorrow?'

2. Closed/Thought: 'Has it rained today?'

3. Open/Experience: 'How did you react when she told you?'

4. Closed/Experience: 'Did you feel nervous at the time?'

In groups where decisions are being made, or a consensus is sought, closed questions may be most appropriate; but in groups where discussion is wanted and opinions and ideas are shared, open questions are more likely to encourage participation.

Questions may be a stumbling block to learning if they are not phrased in the correct way. Sometimes questions are too vague, containing little stimulus for the person who is answering. Consider the following questions:

'What did you learn as a result of last week's
Sunday School training course?'

'What changes will you make as a result of last week's
Sunday School training course?'

Both are valid ways of checking the value of a discipling course but the second one is more pointed, focusing on change rather than the more vague word 'learn'. The second question provides a greater stimulus to think about the past experience.

Questions can be used to encourage learning at different stages of the learning cycle. Here are some examples.

Diagram 5:   **Questions to use at different stages of the learning cycle**

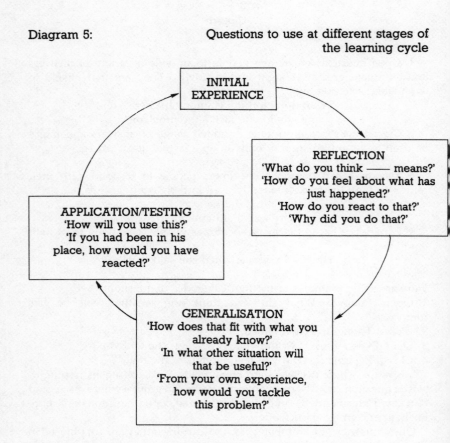

Questionnaires

There are advantages in printing out questions so that people see them written down. These can be used as worksheets representing part of group Bible study or as questionnaires to help people reflect more deeply and personally on a teaching course in which they have participated. Questions in written form allow people the opportunity to think before answering. They may be phrased in order to collect information and opinions, to help people express their feelings, to encourage people to search for faith, or to encourage people to apply what they have learnt.

There are a variety of ways of setting out written questions:

a. Filling in the blank:

Peter _____ before setting out (Bible study)

b. Finishing the sentence:

'The important lesson for me in this discussion is . . . .' (small group worksheet)

'I would like to see more . . . .' (evaluation questionnaire)

c. Placing a cross along a continuum or spectrum line, or circling the appropriate number:

I found the course: Easy _____ Difficult (evaluation questionnaire)

My Christian involvement in the local community is 1   2   3   4   5 (small group worksheet)

d. Straight questions (see section above on asking questions)

e. True or False:

'Which of the following phrases is true or false. . ?'

f. Multiple choice:

'Underline the most appropriate answer. . .'

These are not just gimmicky ways of encouraging an answer but are designed to help people to think more deeply before answering.

Audio-visual aids

Video represents the latest in a wide range of audio-visual aids available to teachers. Churches that cannot afford to buy their own hardware (the machines!) often have access through members of the fellowship. Audio-visual aids are *aids* to learning and can be used to help enhance understanding, prime the memory, encourage concentration by helping to retain interest, or stimulate discussion. They enable communication to occur on more than one level: visual aids adding a visual element to communication, and well produced audio and visual aids may encourage an emotional response to the learning material.

Overhead projectors have tended to replace the blackboard in church halls and Sunday School rooms and may even be in evidence in the worship areas of churches. They have the advantage of being cleaner than chalk and board and can be used without black-out in well-lit rooms. They are adaptable to most sizes of group from the more intimate small group meeting in someone's back room to a church congregation of 200 people. As they rely on a projected image the size of visual aids can be increased by moving the projector further from the screen. Screen size then becomes the only major limiting factor. Transparencies of very high quality can be home-produced by tracing around maps and line drawings in books, or by using a heat copier with special transparencies that enable illustrations to be transferred directly from published material. (Be careful about copyright.) Diagrams and pictures can also be built up by laying one transparency on another (for more details see booklist in Resources section). If transparencies are to be an effective aid they need to be uncluttered and clear – too much detail, particularly when used in large groups, can reduce their impact and value. When using a projector during a talk it helps to turn the machine off when not referring to diagrams – this helps to prolong the life of the bulb and retains the impact of the visuals each time it is turned on.

A projector can be used during a talk or sermon to indicate the main heading, or as a reminder of what has already been said. Those with some artistic flair may draw diagrams, pictures or cartoons as they talk, to illustrate the different points. Commercially produced maps, tables and diagrams can be used to provide historical and geographical context to what is being said. Remember to refer directly to any item on the OHP at the appropriate time, by using a pointer or piece of card – the value of the aid is lost if it is left on the screen without specific attention being drawn to it.

In house groups, discussion groups, training courses, or committees the OHP can be used to display information in the form of diagrams and headings and will be a useful aid for the leader who wants to set the context or provide a stimulus for discussion. It is also a valuable means of displaying summaries of discussions or varieties of answers to a particular question.

'Intergenerational' teaching activities can also benefit from using the OHP for a visual display of instruction that both children and adults will understand and that will help them to carry out an exercise or project. It can also be used to illustrate a talk, providing an added dimension to the words. Children who may not understand all that is said will then glean something from the pictures.

Audio-casettes of talks, music, drama, debates, interviews or a combination of these can make good discussion starters. They do, however, have the disadvantage of providing no visual focus at all. Whereas during a live sermon the listener can focus on the speaker (who may be interesting to watch as well as listen to), in a room with a tape recorder eyes may wander everywhere, desperately searching for something to latch on to. In my experience many adults find it extremely difficult to concentrate on a cassette for any length of time. This can be overcome by dividing listening time into eight- to ten-minute sections, at the end of which the recorder is switched off, a recap made on an overhead projector and, if appropriate, discussion can take place. Alternatively the group may be provided with a 'hand-out' on which the headings of the talk are printed. Where cassettes make use of well produced drama items, listeners may feel themselves being drawn into the action, experiencing emotional as well as intellectual reactions.

Cassettes are ideal for small or medium-sized groups, but many cassette players do not have sufficient amplification for large rooms. Where recordings are to be played back in rooms with poor acoustics, the addition of a separate speaker or amplifier will be required. An increasing range of commercially produced cassettes exists for discussion groups and to aid training groups.

Films/soundstrips. These remain one of the most popular visual aids in churches and do provide an excellent way of communicating information – doctrine, history, story, practical life-issues – imaginatively to both large and small groups.

A soundstrip can be used instead of a talk and is often more effective as it involves the learner at a variety of levels (visual, sound, and feelings). The soundstrip itself may incorporate a variety of techniques to enhance communication, including cartoons, humour, diagrams, tables, vivid colour, and symbolic representations that help people to remember what they have seen. In one excellent soundstrip the inadequacy of mankind is symbolised by the use of masks that people use to cover up their true selves – a vivid symbol that makes a deep impression on many who see it.

Sets of slides and filmstrips, with or without spoken commentary, can all be used to provide background to talks, projects or studies. There are excellent slides of the Holy Land that could provide a stimulus to a series of studies. Discussion can be stimulated by using filmstrips designed to be open-ended so that the group has to think out its own conclusions and apply the learning to itself. In selecting filmstrips and soundstrips remember to check to see for what sort of audience it was designed and if possible preview it to ensure that it will meet the needs of the group with whom you wish to use it.

Video is rapidly becoming the most dominant item in the audio-visual media. In time it may completely replace the filmstrip. Amongst the advantages are its ability to present a more sophisticated programme, and its ease of use, requiring no threading, hand operation, or blackout. At the moment video is a small-group teaching tool ideal for the house group meeting in someone's home; but as technology improves large video projector screens will be available to churches, so that large groups can be accommodated comfortably.

Many of the commercially produced videos portray no more than an individual giving a talk or sermon, so in terms of effectiveness may fit between a tape recording and a live sermon (although the benefits of having outside expertise and dynamic speakers may be helpful for some groups). More imaginatively produced programmes use a documentary style and compare favourably with television documentaries. Videos fulfil a similar function to the filmstrip in discussion groups, training events and for communicating information.

It is important that the hypnotic effect of the more sophisticated media doesn't detract from the use of simpler, and sometimes more effective, visual aids. These may be wall charts and maps that can be pinned up and referred to at learning sessions; flipcharts that can be used to record points of a discussion; and photographs or diagrams that can be handed out to each member of a small group and used to encourage a response or explain an abstract idea during a talk. All these are valuable aids and the key to success is to find the aid (sophisticated or simple) that best furthers the purpose of the group. A good aid to learning provides something for the learners to respond to or reflect on, or acts as an encouragement to application. All audio-visual aids are passive means of promoting learning and need to be used in conjunction with other techniques to ensure that the learning cycle is completed. Having a congregation glued to a TV set or a film screen in a darkened room will do little to develop a learning community! People must be given an opportunity to react to the visual aid and to inter-react with others who have shared the experience. That could be in the form of discussion or using role play or one of the other more active methods included in this chapter.

Open discussion

Open discussion is a learning method for which there is no pre-planned outcome. In other words, the answers to questions or solutions to problems have not been worked out in advance. The stimulus used to get the discussion going – questions, an audio-visual aid, a case study or whatever – is open ended. Open discussion can take place in a number of different contexts within a church setting: a church committee (trying to find the solution to a problem concerning the fabric of the building, the future pattern for worship or a way of ensuring more effective pastoral care); the leaders of the women's groups considering next year's programme; the house group discussing how the studies in the book of James apply to the lives of group members. Open discussion has tremendous value as a tool for learning – everyone can contribute their thoughts, ideas, experiences without fear of not having the right answer. It can be very creative in throwing up solutions/answers not envisaged by the person leading the group. It encourages peer learning (learning from equals), reducing reliance on the leader/'expert'.

Open discussion requires good leadership if it is to be helpful to people. The leader's role involves the following:

1 Providing a clear definition or description of the topic under discussion – making sure it really is an open topic and not one for which the leader requires certain answers.

2 Providing the initial stimulus to discussion that will encourage people to participate – this might involve starting discussion off in pairs or with a questionnaire, using an audio visual or a real live case study or problem. It certainly means using open questions (see section on asking questions).

3 Encouraging the free flow of discussion, without constant interventions by the leader. Each comment doesn't have to be directed at the leader, discussion should be encouraged to flow freely across the group from person to person.

4 Permitting silences during the discussion time without feeling the need to fill them in with his/her own statements or further questions.

Silence can be used constructively to allow people to think and digest what has already been said.

5 Controlling the pace of the discussion – slowing it down if it seems to be going too fast: 'Could we go back to Mr Jones' comment? I'm not sure if we considered it very fully; would others like to react to it?'
Or speeding it up if it gets bogged down.

6 Helping people to listen and reply to each other's comments so that members learn to respond to each other.

7 Encouraging understanding of what has been said: 'Could you explain that again, Jane? I'm not sure whether we all grasped it the first time', or:
'Do you mean . . . ?'

8 Summarising the main elements of the discussion or the conclusions reached. This may be at various points in the discussion, but particularly at the end.

9 Planning time for a 'so what?' at the end of the discussion when the group can look at the implications of their discussion in terms of future action.

10 Refraining from imposing their own ideas on the group, but waiting until everyone else has had the opportunity to contribute.

11 Handling the different personalities in the group so that the discussion benefits from the wide range of experiences and opinions, and is constructive. This means a degree of sensitivity to the different people in the group and an ability to help:
the over-talkative
the excessively critical
the non-participator
the cynic or the joker
'the expert'
the saboteur who wants to disrupt the group.

Ice-breakers

When people come together in a new group or at the start of a new course there is often a degree of uneasiness, even among those who know each other relatively well. Ice-breakers are short exercises designed to unfreeze people in such situations. by encouraging:
● informal mixing, ● participants to make simple contributions so they can hear the sound of their own voices, ● the completion of some simple task that produces a sense of achievement, ● physical movement, ● the relaxing of tension through laughter and fun, ● participants to get to know one or two others in more depth.

Ice-breakers vary in design depending on the needs of the people in the group and the nature of the event. Some are designed to introduce people to the course or session by taking up the theme of the session. Others may be designed for groups who are not used to participation or sharing, encouraging the barriers of embarrassment and shyness to be broken down. A third type of ice-breaker may help to bring strangers together who are going to work with each other for a short time. Ice-breakers may be verbal: people sharing information; or physical: like a game or football or basketball. They may be used at the start of conferences, houseparties, or at the beginning of a new session after Christmas or the summer holidays when people have been apart for some weeks.

Example: 'Expectations'
(To encourage those attending a session to share their expectations of the event.)

1 Ask course participants to divide into pairs and to share with their partner the questions outlined on the OHP (or blackboard or flipchart). Tell them they have 15 minutes to share their answers.
2 The questions displayed (those below were designed for a meeting of Sunday School teachers in a church):
a. What do you enjoy most about working with children?
b. Can you think of any really comical moments in your contact with children (words, incident etc.)? If you can't think of any don't worry.
c. What is the worst experience you have had, or the most difficult part of the work?
d. What do you need to improve your work with children?
e. What do you hope to gain from today's course?
3 Ask each pair to join up with one other pair. Then, in fours, ask each person to briefly state one or two things from conversation with their partner.
4 You may use the list of items from question e. to plan the day's course.

Example: 'Four Quaker Questions'
(This is for new groups where members haven't met before or for groups where people find sharing difficult. This exercise usually works well with older people who are pleased to talk about the past.)

1 In pairs or fours ask people to share memories of the four topics outlined below. Give time for 3 minutes' sharing after each question is spoken by the course leader.

- Where did you live when you were about seven years old?
- How was your house heated when you were seven?
- What was the centre of warmth for you at that age? (a person, a place, a pet or toy) – someone or somewhere that you went to for security?
- When did God first become warm to you? When did he become real?

2 If done in pairs, pairs may introduce each other and each others' experiences to another pair.

Example: 'Collage'
(Using a visual means of communicating information, followed by words – some people find this an easier way to work. Ideal for a small group but it has worked with two hundred.)

1 Give each participant a piece of plain paper about 12″ × 18″, a pile of magazines, and a container of gum or paper glue.
2 Tell everyone that they are going to be asked to share something of their lives with others using pictures and words torn from the magazines. They should divide up their 'message' into *past*, *present* and *future*. They may divide the sheet of paper into three if they wish (of equal or unequal size).
3 Pictures and words should be found that say something about their past – anything they wish (home, family, experiences, school, job etc); their present (Christian experience, work, joys, sorrows etc); their future (hopes, fears, plans, uncertainties).
4 After 10 to 15 minutes invite people to share their collages with others around them, guessing what others have said about themselves and chatting about their own.

Symbolism

The Bible is full of symbolism. Jesus made frequent use of symbolism – bread and wine representing his suffering and death, water to represent spiritual life, yeast to represent the presence of evil. Elsewhere in the Bible we read of the Holy Spirit appearing in symbolic form as a dove, fire and wind. The Bible itself is symbolised by a sword. The value of symbolism for both Jesus and other writers was that it made things that were unseeable or abstract more real to those being taught, because they were represented by something concrete. Adults today are no different from those that Jesus spoke to in that the concrete image is more easily understood and remembered than the abstract concept. It is worth remembering this especially when preparing talks and sermons, where communication relies heavily on words.

In today's church symbolism is often either avoided, as if it were tantamount to idolatry, or its forms are so outdated that those involved with it have forgotten its true meaning and fail to benefit from it. Symbolism primarily involves the substitution of concrete and tangible images for one important idea or experience, in order to aid our understanding and memory.

Biblical symbols were objects and actions that had relevance to the lives of ordinary people. Jesus himself used everyday things and we need to ensure that our symbolism is up-to-date. By using familiar items encountered by people in their daily lives Christians can be helped in their learning and hence in their discipleship. The symbol doesn't have to be an object like the bread and the wine; it can be an action like a hug at the door representing our caring and concern for someone. A touch on the shoulder or arm of someone sharing something painful in a house group symbolises identification with the pain.

Example: Symbolism in an Easter service

A colleague of mine taking a church service at Easter asked sidesmen to give out small stones to everyone coming in to the service. During the sermon he asked everyone to hold up their stones and said, 'Your stone is like the stone that was placed across Jesus's tomb in an attempt to keep his body there – it failed. When you go home today I would like you to place your stone against the stem of a plant growing in your house or garden, one that you will notice each day. As the growing life of your plant is not stopped by the stone resting on it remember that the resurrection of Jesus broke through the stone that sealed his tomb and that he lives today, just like your plant.'

A very simple illustration and symbolic act, but it had a remarkable effect. An amazing number of people came to my colleague weeks later and said how they still looked at the stone against the plant as they went out each morning and were prompted to thank God for Jesus.

Analogies

Analogies and symbols are closely related as they both enable people to make sense of, and express, their faith. Analogies are verbal or mental pictures that help to bring issues of faith into concrete expression. Instead of focusing on their use in teaching we will look at how we can use analogy to help people express their faith in discussion.

We have considered how adults find it difficult to express their emotions and I have found it helpful to encourage them to think of the way they feel in terms of more concrete things like colours or music. Colours are used to express emotions in songs, paintings and even in everyday speech (feeling 'blue', green with envy, red with embarrassment). It is interesting to ask adults what colour they would use to represent the character of God as they see it. Many would say white or gold to represent his holiness and glory, some might say red or purple and link this with his authority or position as judge. This is not the usual way of encouraging adults to express themselves and may be approached rather 'tongue-in-cheek' by some adults, but in my experience most of these people are amazed at the discussion and discoveries that result from such a starting point.

Example: Analogy to describe relationship with God

Ask your confirmation group, baptismal class, church membership group or house group to think about their relationship to God right now and to represent it with a piece of music – do they feel like the 'Hallelujah Chorus' or more like 'Blues in the night'? If music is too difficult then get them to choose a colour. For those who have never done this before give them some examples to choose from rather than a completely free choice and share your own feelings in this way first as a sign of your sincerity.

Example: Analogy to explore self-perception

In the Scripture Union Training Unit we have used similar techniques when training people for lay ministry. One aspect of this training has been to help participants be aware of how they see and value themselves. Initially this can be an embarrassing topic to discuss, but we have got round this by asking members of courses to choose a car that represents how they think about themselves, their abilities, their personalities. For example, do they see themselves as:

- a new, fast Porche sports car, which makes progress at a fantastic rate, impatient with slower cars on the road?
- a nineteen-fifties Ford Popular which has really had its day, a few cobwebs under the seats, not as fast as it used to be, a little bit temperamental?

This exercise invariably creates a lot of laughs but ends with some personal discoveries and serious discussion that is usually of great value to the participants. The use of the analogy can often make people think more deeply about issues that are familiar.

Silence

Unless we fill every minute of our teaching time with words we may feel that the time has been wasted. Silence in meetings can be uncomfortable for some, a diversion to others and helpful to those who know how to use it. The majority of Protestant churches are not very well versed in the use of silence and yet it is a valuable means of encouraging thought. Here we will concentrate on the use of silence during a talk or discussion group rather than during worship, where it may also be used to great effect.

A period of silence lasting from a few seconds to minutes can help people consider their answers to questions posed, or to reflect on their past and present experiences, or digest and react to things already said or discussed. In every discussion group there will be some adults who are not very good at producing instant answers and comments, and often by the time they have thought of what they want to say, the discussion has moved on making their contribution irrelevant. These people need space in which to think. Silence can be introduced into a discussion to slow the pace, encouraging people to consider current contributions more thoroughly before moving on to new avenues.

Most people, however, need help in using silence. This can be accomplished by structuring silences and providing participants with something to focus on during the silence – a question, a problem, a situation, a reading, or description.

Here are some examples:

Example: Use of silence during sermon/talk

In the sermon the preacher asks people to think about how they would react in a particular situation and gives them time to think; *or* he asks them to consider particular things from their past experience (eg. when they first realised God was real) and gives space for thought.

Example: Use of silence in house group Bible study

In the house group the leader suggests five minutes' thinking time after asking the first question, inviting members to write things down for discussion. The leader encourages people to look through a Bible passage in silence for a while noting anything they don't understand or that challenges them, ready for sharing later.

Sometimes it is the teacher or leader who needs help in handling silence. House group leaders may feel uncomfortable when there is silence in a group and may be tempted to fill every space with a comment or another question. A speaker may feel that he is not using his limited time in the most profitable way if he encourages silent thought. These people can be helped by first making them aware of their own reactions to silence and then showing them how to use silence constructively.

Hand-outs

Hand-outs are simply printed or duplicated sheets containing information that needs to be in the hands of everyone present at a meeting – the agenda for a committee, questions for a discussion or Bible study group, the main points of a talk or sermon. We've already considered the use of questionnaires so here we focus on the use of other types of hand-outs. For adults who find it hard to concentrate, or whose memory is 'not all it used to be', hand-outs can be invaluable. But they can also simply become extra pieces of paper floating around the church, so do think about their use and usefulness before running off reams on the church duplicator. They probably have their greatest value when used to summarise material covered during a series of talks or a short course, when it is hoped that participants will continue to learn by referring back to notes at a later stage. Such an occasion may be a training course for the pastoral team or house group leaders, a special study course in the book of James, a course on parenthood for new parents, a preparation course on evangelism, a day's teaching on how to use the Bible.

Hand-outs should be produced as attractively as possible – not cramming too many lines of print on a page, using good clear page layout, and illustrations, diagrams or cartoons to convey information/ideas.

They can be designed in a number of ways:

1 To give major headings of a talk or presentation with space beneath each heading for people to make notes during the session. This is an aid to concentration and memory and gives people something to do during an otherwise passive learning session.

2 To note the major points of a talk, the sheet being given out at the beginning and referred to at regular intervals, or distributed at the end as a reminder to take away.

3 A worksheet/questionnaire to fill in during the session.

4 An instruction sheet to help a group carry out their own project or to enable them to work independently of a teacher. This is particularly useful when there are a limited number of leaders and some form of involvement or practical work is required.

5 A summary of the main conclusions from a previous week's meeting, outlining conclusions reached or points made. This may then be used as a starting place for continued discussion.

Those who use hand-outs need to know before they see it when the hand-out is going to be given out and how it is to be used. The latter should be clearly explained.

Guided meditation

For some the word meditation conjures up images of eastern religions and sitting in peculiar positions. Meditation need not be linked with other religious practices; it is simply a discipline of thinking which enables people to focus their thoughts on particular subjects, ideas, feelings or experiences. Guided meditation may be used during a talk or as part of a group meeting. By encouraging people to enter more intimately into the topics under consideration it helps the learning process. It can be used to help people to remember in detail particular experiences with their accompanying feelings or to imagine more vividly situations which are not part of their experience.

The essence of a guided meditation is that the teacher/leader takes people through the meditation by describing situations in detail and inviting people to answer questions in their mind, or to visualise scenes or experience events, providing periods of silence in between the promptings for people to meditate.

Many find it easier to meditate with their eyes closed, relaxing in an easy-chair, but these elements are not essential.

Example: Guided meditation to recall past feelings

In a course on 'Being a Christian parent' a leader wanted those present to think about their own childhood, so she asked them to close their eyes, relax and to think back to when they were seven or eight (the precise age didn't matter). She then guided them into the memory by suggesting things to remember concentrating on feelings as well as events and providing plenty of time between each item to help them:

- think of the house you are living in, go round the rooms in turn.
- Is there a special room or place where you like to be?
- Who's living in the house with you – people and pets?
- What happens when you're naughty? Who punishes you and what do they do?
- Who plays with you most and what do you play?
- Who lives on either side and how do you feel towards them?

The periods of silence are there so that people can 'live out' again in their minds the experiences of their past.

The meditation was followed by discussion, leading on to look at the way our own upbringing affects the way we raise our own children.

Example: Guided meditation to imagine a biblical scene

In another teaching course a house group leader took members through the story of Mary Magdalene discovering the empty tomb and then meeting Jesus. With eyes closed he described the scene getting people to imagine they were there and experiencing the loneliness, and later the joy, of Mary – again using silences to allow people to experience in their imaginations what it was like. This introduction to a study of the Bible passage produced more animated discussion than the group had ever had before.

Brainstorming

This is a very simple method of helping people in a small group to be creative in thinking up solutions to problems or answers to open questions, and can create a vast amount of material for later discussion. The rules of brainstorming are as follows:

In a predetermined period of time (10 minutes or so) group members make a list of as many answers/solutions/ideas that they can think of. Someone writes up this list for all to see. Anyone can contribute, but their contribution should be short and to the point. There is *no* discussion of any item. Everything is written down, even 'way out' suggestions. When the time period is up the list can then be sorted out, putting similar items together and working out an order of priority for discussion. Then discussion of the suggestions takes place. The discussion is a vital follow-up to the brainstorming but it comes right at the end.

Brainstorming can be used in a house group to collect ideas for future study. It can also be used in a training group as a means of looking at ways of handling a situation – for instance, 'how would you handle the adult who is shy and won't take part?' Before discussing the problem in depth, list all possible solutions.

Problem-solving exercise

Much of research into adult learning shows that adults are problem-centred in their learning. In other words they develop most of their new insights, behaviour, attitudes etc. when confronted with problems that they have to overcome – learning to use a new machine, a new procedure for claiming benefit, bringing up the first child, finding a route, knowing what to say when someone challenges their faith.

In our teaching we can use problem situations to help adults learn about, and apply, their faith.

Example: Presenting the gospel

An illustration of this is taken from a teaching course devised by a church just outside London. The aim was to help adult Christians in their understanding of basic doctrine. After a 15-minute talk on some aspect of doctrine (eg. the nature of God) the course was divided into small groups of five or six and each was given a large card on which there was illustrated different characters they might meet in their community (a typical next-door-neighbour, a child, a teenager, an office worker, a mechanic, someone inside the church, someone outside the church). The job of the group was to work out how they would translate what they had heard about the nature of God into terms/words that their character could understand.

In tackling this problem the members of each group had to think over what they had heard (checking that they all had the same understanding); decide on the essentials that had to be communicated; think about the person they were communicating to and what would aid their understanding; and put their interpretation into a relevant form. This is an excellent way of helping adults put their understanding of the Christian faith to practical use, reinforcing their understanding at the same time.

The key to problem-solving is to devise a situation that will be realistic to the participants. It may be an incident or event or a task to complete. The problem may be written out on slips of paper or described verbally. Problem-solving could be used as part of a group Bible study, training session, specialist teaching group, or at the end of a talk, and is ideal for helping people apply knowledge to their lives.

Case studies

Example: A marriage in difficulty

A minister wanting to make a training session for members of his pastoral team true to life commenced his day course with a detailed example of a problem that he had been confronted with. He painted a detailed picture of Mr and Mrs Jones whose only teenage son had just left home for university; how they had put a lot of time and energy into bringing up this son even though the latter years had been difficult, the parents having to deal with a lot of rebellion and rejection.

Now alone, the two were finding each other's company a strain and the marriage seemed to be drifting apart. Whereas both had attended a home group in the past now only one came, their joint attendance at church services also declined and they admitted to Christian friends that they frequently argued or spent long periods in silence at home.

This detailed situation was a case study, based on a real situation but disguised to conceal the identity of those involved. The pastoral team were first asked to identify their feelings towards the three people involved – husband, wife, son – and then to work at ways of helping this couple when they came for help. This case study set the scene for considering principles and skills in pastoring.

Case studies are simply detailed examples based on real situations that help to make teaching and training more concentrated for the listeners, or help people to apply principles to real situations. Besides use in a teaching or training situation, they may be used as a way of applying lessons learned, or as examples, during talks or sermons. The secret is to make the case study as near as possible to real events that the hearers can identify with.

Example: Presenting the gospel to a specific family

As part of a teaching course on sharing the Good News, participants were given a printed description of a family. The individual personalities, background, values, pastimes, lifestyle and circumstances of the family were described (this matched a typical family living in the actual neighbourhood). Members of the teaching group were divided into fours and asked to suggest where the Good News had relevance to this family and how a Christian friend might start to share the Good News with them.

Role play

This is a method that encourages people to think about how others react and behave in particular situations. It is a very valuable tool in making people more sensitive and aware of these actions and reactions.

Example: Reactions and interactions of a family

During a three-evening course on coping with teenagers for a group of sixteen parents of teenagers in a church, the course leader wanted to help people to understand more about the tussles that occur when teenagers demand more freedom in the way they live.

He asked the course to divide into fours. One person was to play mother, one father, one the 'rebellious' son or daughter and the other either a younger brother or sister or a grandparent living with the household. The scene was set: breakfast time – three at the table eating breakfast, 'rebellious' son/daughter still to arrive. Tension mounts as the three at table wait because son/daughter was late in the night before, having been warned on previous occasions that late nights must stop as school work was suffering. The rebellious teenager is now late for breakfast and will be late for school.

Each character has a description of their role which they have to be true to (eg. Dad tends to leave discipline to Mum because he's so busy at work; Mum is worried by a spate of rapes/vandalism in the town and the type of people wandering the streets at night, as well as the suffering school work; the teenager wants freedom like his/her friends, whose parents put fewer restrictions on them, and is angry that he/she is not trusted). Each group of four then act out the scene to themselves. The teenager enters the 'room' and the dialogue is worked on the spot. So without any practice each role player must act out the character they have been allocated.

A role play may last 2–5 minutes and when the action dries up or has run its course the leader stops the action and leads a discussion on what happened, with questions like:
• How did people feel playing their role? • Were they realistic characters? • Were the reactions of individuals realistic? • Why did people react the way they did? • What alternative ways are there of solving the problems?
The role play may be acted out with people simply sitting around a table with very little in terms of action.

This is an ideal method for involving people in learning. It provides an actual experience that has an emotional dimension as well as stimulating thoughts. When participants enter into their role they begin to experience real emotional reactions to the situation and to other characters. It works best with behaviour/relationship topics when you want people to understand the relationship/behaviour and the emotions that go with them.

Of all the methods used to date, this is a more total learning experience than any other mentioned. It requires the learners to take more risks but pays higher dividends in terms of learning than many more passive teaching methods.

Demonstration
This is teaching by providing people with a practical example of 'how it should be done'. On a course on door-to-door visiting the teacher gave an actual demonstration of what to do when someone answers the door, acting it out in the church hall and asking for comments on the good and bad points at the end of the demonstration. In a teaching series taking place over Easter, one church asked a group to act out the Jewish passover meal during their midweek fellowship meeting, as a way of helping its members to understand the point of the Last Supper. During a training course for home group leaders the trainer/teacher demonstrated how to lead a Bible study by actually doing a Bible study with a group of volunteers in the church lounge while the others watched and made notes of positive and negative aspects of the leadership.

Demonstration involves showing people how something works (acting out an event etc.) or how something should be done. When demonstrating the latter the idea is not to make the observers feel there is no room for criticism – the teacher must not set himself up as perfect. Adults do not find criticism easy and some leaders may be reticent to open themselves to a process that might, in their eyes, lead to disrespect for their authority.

Show and tell
People often find it difficult to put their thoughts, views, feelings into words, either because they don't know how to express these things in words, or because they need time to think before they respond, or because they are fearful of what others will think of their contribution. One way round this is to encourage a more indirect and hence safer way of contributing to discussion. It involves asking people to think about their answer and to represent it in the form of a drawing, diagram, analogy or model. It enables people to express their feelings (as well as thoughts) in a concrete way, often by using symbols.

1. Using a graph to recount Christian experience
In a teaching course on evangelism a group of adults were asked to share their own Christian experience. Instead of simply sharing in words they were first asked to draw it as a graph; the peaks on the graphs representing the high points in their Christian lives, for instance, when they first responded to God, their baptism/confirmation, a Christian conference, a testing time when God was very real to them.

2. Modelling the church
At the beginning of a teaching session on The Church, the members of a house group were each given a piece of plasticine and asked to model it into a shape that said something about how they saw the church in this country. This produced various objects including a heart-shape representing love in the community and a series of disconnected blobs from someone who felt the church was disorganised and unco-ordinated. Models were shared and talked about and studies on Ephesians and I Corinthians followed.

3. Using montage
After a Bible teaching series on the Holy Spirit a midweek fellowship was asked to divide into groups of eight and to summarise what they had learned about the Holy Spirit by producing montages made up from magazine pictures and words. Dividing the page in two they used one half to portray their understanding of the Holy Spirit before the study, and on the other half the things they had learned during the study. Again this involved using symbols – a picture of a fire or wind blowing through trees.

After the study the pictures and images remained in the participants' minds longer than words shared in ordinary discussion.

When asked to take part in this type of learning exercise some adults may hold back or even resist. Participants can be gently encouraged, with the leader trying it out as well. Many who have been introduced to this type of exercise have discovered a new dimension to their learning.

Values clarification

This is a method used to help people think about the things they value and the priorities they have in their own lives. It usually involves asking people to choose from a list of values *or* to grade priorities from a list provided.

Example: Why do church members value their church?

During a teaching session on the church participants were asked to list three things that they valued most about belonging to their church. They were asked to choose from a list provided:

good teaching _____
somewhere to go on Sunday _____
a place to meet people like me _____
a place to use my gifts _____
a feeling of warmth and acceptance _____
fulfilling worship _____
care and support _____
a good minister _____
they care for my children _____
other _____
other _____
other _____

Space was given for people to add other items if they wished.

Sharing and discussion followed on the ways different participants valued their church and the reason for these. Study of the nature of the church in Romans 12 concluded the session.

Example: Priority of aims in a house group

In a training session for house group leaders each was given a list of eight aims of a house group and were asked to put these in order of priority for their own groups:

to study the Bible _____
to have fellowship _____
to provide pastoral care _____
to worship _____
to build relationships _____
to encourage learning _____
to be a centre for evangelism _____
to share experiences of life _____
other _____

The aim of this method of teaching is to help Christian adults to become aware of their values and priorities so that, if necessary, they can be challenged (by teacher, peer, self) and then changed. Where a training or teaching course starts with this exercise it might also conclude with a similar exercise so that people can identify how their thinking has changed as a result – a good way of illustrating that change is part of the learning process.

Simulation exercises

A number of years ago one missionary society brought out a board game, played with counters and dice and taking the players around a track that helped them to understand some of the joys and frustrations of being a missionary with that particular society. As players entered into the game, not only did they share some of the burdens and experiences of Christian work overseas, but they also acquired a lot of knowledge of how the society worked. Board games have grown in popularity over the last ten years, not just among children, but among adults and whole families. *Monopoly* once monopolised the shop shelves, but, there are now a confusing array of games to choose from. Some are abstract in design but many attempt to simulate real life situations in the world of business, banking, exploration, travel, crime detection and the natural world. As well as the commercial games, there is an even greater variety of educational games that never appear in shops but are played regularly in schools to help children understand ideas and processes in almost every subject taught. In adult education games are used extensively to teach managers, health workers, social workers, and teachers themselves. Whether you describe these as games or prefer the more respectable description 'exercises', these are all attempts to simulate the real world, enabling those involved to get fully involved, but in the safety of their homes (or classrooms). When used properly they are a very powerful teaching tool because they include a high level of participation for the 'players'. They also involve players emotionally as well as mentally in their experience of the real world.

Simulation exercises may involve a playing board and action cards (like Monopoly) or may involve activity and role playing by participants like Christian Aid's, 'Trading Game'.

Example: The Trading Game

The Trading Game is an excellent example of the use of simulation in Christian teaching and learning, as it simulates the inequality between nations and encourages people to appreciate the needs and frustrations of the Third World, emotionally and mentally. Players take on the roles of different nations with varying amounts of wealth, expertise and natural resources. The game requires that these nations trade in order to meet their country's needs.

The frustration of having raw materials but no expertise, or money and no raw materials, soon emerges and the feelings mount as the exercise progresses.

Games are not easy to design, though. The easiest are simple board games with action cards that provide information and instructions as the game progresses. There are books on the design of simulation exercises; some are included in the reference section at the end of this book. Beginners may prefer to try out exercises that already exist and that have been published (again see the reference section).

In playing 'The Trading Game' mentioned above, with adult groups there may be some initial embarrassment from those who have never participated in this sort of teaching session before. When I've used the game it has made a startling impact and on one occasion a group were so challenged by the experience that they committed themselves to an action plan. When people do not want to participate in the game they can be asked to be observers, watching the progress of the game and noting what actually happens. This in itself is a very valuable role and benefits both the observer and the players – who may get so engrossed that they lose their objectivity. Simulation games, because of their relative complexity, rely on the skills of the teacher/leader who must understand and explain the rules clearly; watch the progress of the exercise (stepping in if things get out of hand); and decide when to bring the game or exercise to a close. The game is followed by discussion to help reflect on, and consolidate, the experience. It should focus on people's feelings, reactions and behaviour during the game. During the discussion participants are invited to compare the game with what they know of real life, and to share any new information or understanding gained during the exercise. The final element of discussion should enable people to think about the implications of the experience for their own lives.

If you have never experienced this type of learning exercise, try to place yourself at the receiving end before using a game with others.

Experiential exercises

In this chapter we've progressed from fairly passive learning and teaching experiences to those that encourage more involvement physically, mentally and emotionally and that attempt to bring the real world of being a disciple into the 'classroom'. The role of the teacher has also been changing; in earlier methods the teacher is prominent, providing information and expertise (taking the traditional teaching role). In later methods the teacher's role has changed to that of guide, helping people to explore, to express themselves, and to reflect. In this technique there is the minimum of 'interference' from the teacher and a maximum of participation from the learner. Experiential exercises actually recreate real life experiences in the 'classroom' from which people can learn something they can then apply to other real life situations. These exercises are the hardest to describe in writing but can be one of the most effective means of formal learning – because they come closest to informal experiences. At the same time, the outcomes of such exercises are less predictable than other methods of teaching and this has to be accepted by the teacher.

We use experiential exercises quite extensively in the work of the Training Unit as we train people for ministry, and although exercises can be used for a variety of learning needs I have chosen to illustrate from the world of training – in fact the training of those involved in teaching adults in the local church.

Example: communication exercise

In order to help adults think about the way they communicate the Bible to other adults, we adapted a simple communication exercise:

> Those attending the training course were asked to form threes and each three was asked to label themselves A, B, C. A's were stationed at one end of the room and were given a relatively simple lego model which they were asked to keep concealed at all times. B's were stationed in the middle of the room and C's were stationed at the opposite end of the room to the A's; they also had lego pieces but not made up into a model. The object of the exercise was for A to communicate the model to C so that C could made an exact replica. A had to communicate via B, never directly with C.

So in order to teach about communication we actually gave people something 'real' to communicate – we set up the communication process in the 'classroom'. Before the exercise began more rules were added. A and B could only describe the model in words – no diagrams or visual aids could be used. But B could ask A questions as A described the model. C could not ask anything as B attempted to repeat the description.

At the end of the time allocated the models were compared and the trios shared thoughts and feelings. The discussion focused on the actual experience before attempting to relate it to the way we try communicating God's word.

As stated earlier it is not possible to predict fully what people will learn. Some C's become very frustrated because they can't tell B how confused they are, or how well they are doing. B's might be annoyed with A's because they try and tell them too much or use terms they don't understand. A's may long to be able to use visual aids as they battle with the vagueness of words. Feelings may run high and need to be discussed and not avoided. Few adults need to have the application of the experience spelt out, and discussion often follows with particular focus on the inadequacy of sermons in allowing a response from listeners.

What is significant is that for many who take part in such a learning exercise the information and ideas that emerge are not new, but they do have a new impact because they are *experienced* and not just discussed. This new way of learning has prompted many to go away and act for the first time on things they have known in their minds for a long time.

B. The learning cycle and teaching methods

In order to illustrate the relationship between theory and practice we can now link the learning cycle of chapter three with actual teaching methods, many of which have been described in this chapter.

Providing an experience
Remember that any teaching method, whether it be passive or fully participative, is an experience for the learner. Our aim as teachers or leaders is to provide experiences that help learners become better disciples – extending their discipleship to cover every area of life. We can choose techniques that allow the use of a variety of human senses: • visual aids, • role play, • experiential exercise.

The emotional dimension to learning
Understanding and expressing the emotional side of learning is very difficult for adults generally and usually harder for men than for women. The expression of emotions is much neglected, often because of the fear that they may become uncontrollable, or in fact be irrational. But because emotions are involved in learning we need to learn to recognise the effect they have. Certain methods help us to identify, assess, and express the emotional dimension of learning: • certain types of questions, • symbolism, • analogies, • guided meditation, • role play, • simulation and • experiential exercises.

Supporting flagging concentration
This can be done through the use of • questions, • hand-outs, • audio-visual aids, and almost any activity that involves a high level of participation.

Making the teaching concrete
Instead of assuming that adults can understand abstract ideas we must recognise that many adults, irrespective of their academic achievements, find it hard to grasp abstract ideas and to think abstract thoughts. We need to make every effort to make abstract ideas concrete both by giving and using concrete examples but also by the use of sight and touch in our teaching. Techniques that help include: • audio-visual aids, • symbolism, • analogies, • guided meditation, • case studies.

Helping people to reflect on experience
Most adults actually need to be helped to reflect on teaching provided through formal experiences, and after everyday, informal experiences. This is how we make sense of what God is saying to us. Reflection can be planned into sessions: techniques to consider include: • the use of questions to probe what has already been discovered/learned; • the use of silence structured into teaching sessions with or without guidance on

how to use it to think through issues; • hand-outs that summarise and question things already experienced, discussed, or taught; • 'show and tell' which encourages personal thought before sharing; • values classification; • learning diaries (see p. 100).

Involvement
Despite resistance, sometimes from both teacher and learner, adults need to be involved in their own learning. Passivity breeds passivity. Breaking through that resistance may take some time and needs to be tackled gently. Try out different methods: • open discussion, • problem solving, • role play, • simulation exercises and • experiential exercises.

The importance of reinforcement and application
So often we leave application of teaching/learning subconsciously to chance or consciously to the work of the Holy Spirit. We need to do far more to help learners to see how they can apply things learnt in one situation to another and how learning involves actual change in behaviour, attitudes and understanding. We can encourage this process through: • asking questions, • a questionnaire, • open discussion, • analogies, • problem solving, • case studies, • values classification, and • experiential exercises.

Creating a climate for learning
Because learning is not always easy for adults and may at times be uncomfortable, a climate of acceptance, caring and support helps to create the security that is needed for people to take risks. Adults need to feel comfortable learning in the presence of other adults, especially when greater participation is required. To achieve this, time needs to be taken to build up relationships. Creating the right learning climate also depends to a large extent on the leader/teacher of the group but techniques like ice-breakers can help and the informality of the small group can make participation easier. Fears can also be allayed if proper explanation and consultation takes place. Whatever steps we take to make 'risk-taking' easier we must accept that fears may never be fully removed. Techniques themselves are not guarantees of successful teaching or learning but they are very useful and flexible tools that can assist the learning process. For many adults the new dimensions of learning opened up to them will be a revelation. They may bring excitement and joy to learning for some; for others they may at first bring discomfort and even a little pain. But without a doubt they can be used to encourage adults in their understanding of discipleship and the nature of Christian growth.

Exercise
Consider the teaching you are involved in. How might you incorporate any of the methods outlined in this chapter in order to increase the learning potential for those who participate?

6 Structures for learning

6
Structures for learning

There are many churches that have to live with fixed pews and bare dusty halls; it is part of their heritage. Buildings designed in past eras were not built to cope with the flexibility and rapid change that we have to cope with in the late twentieth century. One of the biggest constraints on introducing new teaching and learning programmes into the church is that the building is designed for the passive, instructed learner. We cannot escape from the fact that the discipling process is closely linked with the context in which it takes place. In this chapter we focus on this context, paying particular attention to ways of grouping adults for teaching and learning and then, more briefly, considering the environment in which they learn.

The place of large groups

The most common teaching unit in the church is still the medium to large group where twenty-five or more people gather for teaching. The most common teaching method used with this group is the talk, sermon or lecture. We would immediately identify the Sunday sermon with this, but mid-week church meetings could also be included, along with large specialist gatherings such as wives' meetings or missionary meetings. It is for this type of teaching that most church buildings are designed.

Large groups have an important part to play in the discipling work of the church and their effectiveness as learning opportunities rests *partly* on the communication skills of the teacher/speaker/preacher – especially on the way they organise and present their material. This use of the large group is effective for the proclamation of truth, for challenging the church family as a whole, for providing a large number of people with the benefits of a gifted preacher or 'expert' in some area of discipleship and for communicating knowledge and information.

The weaknesses of these occasions are that the learners are passive, doing practically nothing other than using their ears; they provide minimal, if any, opportunity for the listeners to 'check out' things they do not understand or to enter into dialogue with the speaker, and often take no account of the listeners' limited concentration span. These weaknesses may be compounded by speakers who are too abstract in the way they present material, failing to use helpful illustrations or anecdotes, or who provide little guidance in how to put their teaching into practice.

In training people to be good preachers or speakers it is important that they are helped to understand the learner as well as the message they communicate. Those who teach and preach should understand the limitations of working with large groups and be encouraged to structure their talks in ways to help people learn. Here are a few suggestions:

Make teaching relevant

People listening to talks and sermons are more likely to prick up their ears if they can see the relevance of what is being taught to their everyday lives. When preparing a talk or sermon a speaker should ask herself some searching questions: ● What sort of lives do my listeners lead? ● What jobs do they do? ● What are their hobbies and pastimes? ● What age groups are represented? ● What is family life like? ● What problems and stresses do they face?

The answers to these questions should provide some insights into appropriate illustrations and examples which should not simply reflect the speaker's world but should touch the experience of the people listening. In medium-sized groups where people know each other specific illustrations may be taken from the lives of the adults listening – with their permission, of course! In this way the teaching is 'earthed' in the real world of the adults present and they can more readily see some of its implications. Obviously, a teacher cannot do this until he knows his listeners and has shared, to some extent, in the ups and downs of their lives. Where this identification is achieved, the teacher's whole approach to sermon preparation will probably be influenced. He may wish to put more emphasis on theme or issue-based preaching, which directly addresses the problems and concerns of the fellowship, than on less direct systematic expositional preaching.

Encourage personal application

In his very stimulating book, *The Church in the Home*, David Prior comments: 'We hear sermon after sermon; we listen to tape after tape; we have Bible study after Bible study and scarcely any of it is put into practice'. One of the reasons for this may be to do with providing insufficient help for our church members in applying the teaching to their lives. Adults need practical suggestions, a challenge, a stimulus and guidelines for action. Sometimes it will mean encouraging the whole church to respond as a group and at other times the application will be aimed at individual response. Although a speaker cannot provide 'so what?' examples that will be relevant to everyone listening, he can offer a selection. He can also encourage people to work more actively at the 'so what?' for themselves, by suggesting a range of options or a spectrum of reactions and inviting listeners to place themselves within the two extremes. Silence in which to digest and respond to such suggestions needs to be incorporated into meetings so that those attending will realise that they really are expected to make a personal response to what has been said. When, however, a speaker moves rapidly from point to point the listener has no time to respond, even internally.

Visual aids

Visual aids need to be used intelligently during a talk if they are to improve learning in the large group meeting. They need to be visible to everyone so that even those with poor eyesight can benefit. More has been written about visual aids in chapter five.

Varying group sizes

Large groups can be broken down into smaller groups, even into pairs, where people can be asked to 'buzz' ideas or discuss answers to a range of questions. Even those sitting in fixed pews can be asked to turn and share their thoughts with a neighbour. Here is an opportunity for individuals to participate and to respond to a speaker so their learning is no longer passive. If this form of involvement is not possible during the talk then opportunity may be found at the end with questions either from speaker to listeners or from listeners to speaker.

Example: Discussing the sermon in small groups
Try this after your next talk or sermon:
'Could you turn to the people sitting on either side of you and in threes
spend five minutes sharing what you feel you've got out of this sermon
– you might mention something new that you've learnt, something that
you've been reminded of, something that you are going to do as a
result of what you've heard. If you feel you've gained nothing then be
honest and say so. Remember you've only got five minutes for your
threesome so don't let one person hog all the time!'

Using written aids

Again, for details you might like to refer back to the section in chapter five
on the use of hand-outs. Remember that when you put a piece of paper into
someone's hand they will start to read it, so take care *when* you give them
out. The best time may be as people are coming into the meeting so that they
can glance at the content before the meeting starts. Using a hand-out that
contains the major headings of the talk with space for note-taking under
each heading can add to the adult's involvement during a talk.

Although large group learning has a place it also has many limitations in
terms of helping adults to grow. Hopefully it will be seen as just *one* of many
contexts in which teaching and learning can occur in the local church.

The importance of small groups

In recent years small groups have proliferated in the church, often being
seen as a place where more adequate pastoral care can take place and closer
relationships be built up. They are also one of the most important contexts
for learning. Some are already used in this way, with Bible study and
discussion being high on the agenda. But unfortunately, many churches do
not design their teaching programme to make the best use of the small
group. For instance, leaders are chosen because of their theological
knowledge or because they have some status in the church, so that
discussion tends to be kept to a minimum while the leader explains the
background and meaning of the study. These leader-centred groups are
often a response to the fear that discussion and sharing opens the door to
error or false teaching. The place of the experienced and gifted *speaker* is,
however, the large group and not in the small group, because the strength
of a small group is that *everybody* can be involved. Each person's experiences
and resources can be at the disposal of others in the group, and the
'intimacy' generated can encourage honest exchange.

Emphasis on personal learning and group growth

The small group is the place where more emphasis can be placed on the learner and the discipling process and where individual and group growth and change can be carefully and lovingly nurtured so that all the pain of growth can be faced and survived.

Development of relationships

A small group is limited to between six and twelve members (many would say the optimum size is between eight and twelve). More than this makes the development of relationships within the group difficult. In such groups a 'climate for learning' can be created. Members need to spend time together doing things other than studying. Relationships need to be built in informal settings such as meals, picnics, coffee evenings, parties, outings etc. Leaders need to know how to conduct discussions and Bible studies in a way that will continue the development of this relaxed and secure atmosphere (see chapter seven).

Risk-taking

These are groups where people can take risks: they can share their experiences, problems, fears, misconceptions. It is here rather than in larger groups that people may respond emotionally to their discipleship – where tears can be shed, excitement and joys be shared, or frustrations and uncertainties faced. In small groups adults can be encouraged to apply what they are learning and the unit is small enough for the members to grapple with 'group learning' where growth is corporate and not just individual. Teaching can be geared to individual needs, and outside specialists/ speakers can be brought in to help explore particular areas of concern, giving opportunity for the group to respond.

Greater participation

Small groups can meet in informal surroundings allowing for more flexibility in the teaching methods used and in the way the time is divided up. Here is the place to experiment with new methods of helping people learn – role play, brainstorming, simulation games. Encouragement to action is easier in smaller groups – where people can be given time to share what they have learned and how it will affect their lives. In small groups growth and change can be supported. Lyman Coleman, a designer of small group Bible study material, likens the small group to a 'weight watchers' meeting where individuals commit themselves to a programme of change and use the rest of the group for support and encouragement in their task. In this way a young couple may share in a home group that they feel God is asking them to take more care of their ageing parents. The group may ask them to suggest positive steps to put this conviction into action and may offer support (moral, practical, prayer) in carrying this out.

In summary we can say that small groups can be very effective structures for discipling when:

1 The leadership is well trained, with an emphasis on skills rather than knowledge.
2 The right climate is created.
3 A variety of participatory methods are used.
4 Programmes are produced imaginatively and are designed to allow the learning cycle to function in the group.

Choice and variety through specialist groups

An individual's commitment to a never-ending group is bound to fluctuate according to their interest in the group's activities or to their changing personal circumstances. Groups once set up don't have to continue *ad nauseam*. The *ad hoc* specialist group can have an important part to play in the discipling programme of the Christian community. These groups may be set up at various times of the year to tackle particular issues or to equip people for particular tasks. They have a fixed duration which could range from one meeting to ten sessions spread over ten consecutive weeks. Because of this limited life they can and should demand a high level of commitment. Such groups might be used to train a group in evangelism; train the Sunday School teachers' team; provide an introductory course in New Testament Greek for non-academics; offer a 'Christian basics' course for new Christians or enquirers; provide an intensive study of Jeremiah; or consider the Christian's involvement in politics or his attitude to leisure. On the other hand it could be a marriage preparation course for a number of engaged couples, or retirement preparation for four or five on the verge of retirement. The advantages of such groups is that they can be set up at fairly short notice, they don't need vast numbers to make them viable, they can be related to people's needs and concerns and, of course, they do not demand unending commitment.

Some churches have structured their mid-week meetings around short specialist teaching and training courses. The church family comes together with a variety of learning activities to choose from, each one lasting four to six weeks. The evening is divided into two one-hour sessions and where children are invited they are catered for by volunteers who opt out of a particular series. Those with young families may only manage one session, but many adults may be involved in two activities in an evening. Those who stay at home to babysit may miss a whole series but are able to opt in when a new set of courses begins.

A similar pattern has been developed in some churches on Sunday, as a form of all-age Sunday School. Children go to their classes for forty minutes and adults also have classes, choosing from a range of teaching and training topics.

Where churches are too small to provide a choice there may be opportunities to link up with neighbouring churches to provide mid-week teaching sessions. Alternatively, small churches may prefer to tackle specialist subjects one at a time, spread out over the year.

Leadership training is again a vital factor in the effective working of these groups. Not all need to be led by experts; some may be able to make use of learning packages produced either commercially or by someone in the church.

Learning as a whole fellowship

If the small group provides a potentially friendly atmosphere in which to learn, the multi-generational group provides a family atmosphere in which learning can take place, one generation enriching another. If the small group breaks the fellowship down into a manageable size, the intergenerational group builds up and integrates. 'Intergenerational' or multi-generational learning must not be equated with the family service, which saw a boom in the 1970's and early 80's but which is much criticised today. Intergenerational activities are those where the different generations are brought together with the intention that there should be *communication and relationship-building across generations*. Initially this involves very carefully structured activities that encourage the generations to mix, so that the teenager, for instance, will talk to and work with a widowed, old-age pensioner and the pre-school child play with a middle-aged spinster. Simply bringing the generations together does not ensure any depth of mixing, as witnessed in the average family service or the church picnic where generations or family-units stick together. Intergenerational activities are designed to provide a more positive encounter between age groups.

Such activities can have a vital influence on children as they see adults learning. This in turn can help children and teenagers to accept that learning and change is expected of adult Christians in the same way that they themselves are expected to 'grow up in Christ'. It also provides a structured situation in which Christ's invitation for adult disciples to humble themselves and learn from a child can be taken seriously by the Christian church today. Learning from children has nothing to do with sentimentality – savouring choice expressions and child-like actions. It involves taking seriously the comments of children in a group discussion or 'chat', and applying some of their uncluttered insights to our adult situations. It involves working and playing with children and teenagers and learning from their behaviour and ours as the generations interact.

As relationships and communication deepens, intergenerational activities can enable the church fellowship to grow as a family and to become more the integrated community that acts as a demonstration of God's kingdom.

The 'teaching spot'

In recent years the Family Service has received a lot of criticism and many church leaders who have used this form because they wanted the whole church family to worship together now feel that the Family Service fails to deliver the goods. The main reason for this failure lies in the traditional 'teaching spot'. The teaching spot in a family service has to be aimed at different ages because of the different levels of understanding and experience. Even the most experienced speakers are stretched in knowing how to address these mixed audiences. Some aim their teaching (language and illustrations) at the children and fall into the danger of providing adults with a child's-eye view of Christianity. Despite what is said about adults enjoying and learning from children's talks there is a real danger that those adults who only attend the family service are never stretched or encouraged to relate the teaching to their adult lives. It may even help to reinforce the wrong idea that learning is for children! A few speakers ignore the children and teenagers present, expecting them to sit quietly through a sermon. This only helps to alienate the younger end of the church family from worship with adults, and prevents them from learning. Some speakers have learnt to present each major point in their teaching in a variety of ways, with a variety of illustrations. So there is something for the young to relate to as well as the teenagers and adults present. Drama, visual aids and vivid illustrations all help to bring this form of intergenerational teaching alive to the wide spectrum of ages.

Small, mixed-age groups

If, however, the local church is going to take intergenerational learning seriously then it must find ways of achieving it in small groups made up of eight to fifteen people of mixed ages. Families may stay together or be allowed to split up and be part of separate groups. This can be an important freedom for any teenagers who feel the need to get away from their parents for a time. Such small groups can be formed when the whole church family meets together, the small groups meeting in the same hall either working completely independently or responding to directions given from one leader at the front. Teaching in these groups should be heavily activity based, allowing a high level of involvement from all participants. Groups may work on projects together researching and preparing displays, collages etc. to show others and to stick on the notice boards. Groups may work around a standard Sunday School lesson plan, looking at an area of teaching together and using craft work, drama, games etc. to express what they have learnt.

Leadership of such groups needs to be in the hands of an adult or a teenager who is sufficiently outgoing to communicate the task to the group and to encourage all ages to take part. Adults and children should then work *together*, rather than the adults simply directing the children in what to do.

Opportunities for intergenerational learning may be a regular feature of a fellowship's life, taking place once a month in one of any number of contexts: as part of Sunday morning worship, a Sunday afternoon programme, an early evening mid-week meeting (perhaps integrated into the ideas given in the section on small groups earlier in this chapter), an extended house group meeting once a month where children and even neighbours are invited. Alternatively, intergenerational activities may be a feature of special occasions occurring at intervals throughout the year where the church family gets together to celebrate and learn, for instance, at harvest time, Christmas, or the Church Anniversary.

However frequently intergenerational activities take place they do not replace the need for generations to learn and be taught in peer groups where more specific age-related needs can be addressed.

This glimpse of intergenerational discipling provides a picture of the church as a learning community where everyone is learning and where individuals encourage each other's learning, not just adult to child and adult to adult, but sometimes child to adult. As God's Spirit promotes change and growth in both individuals and the whole church family there develops a real concern and support for each other. Here change is expected and coped with.

Worship and prayer

The learning communities that made up the first church were also worshipping communities. Worship has been a means by which man has responded to what he has discovered and is discovering about God, and a close link must remain between learning and worship. For many adults worship has a strong emotional element; it may not be revealed outwardly, but is nevertheless felt. It is this awareness and communication of strong feelings that is often neglected in other learning experiences for Christians. If Christians can be encouraged to link worship and learning they may also be able to see the connections between emotions and understanding. Praise and thanksgiving takes on a new dimension when it emanates from a new discovery about one's self or about God. Worship in turn may also form a context in which new learning can take place and in which God can reveal himself and his desires in new ways. In worship – as a structured activity or part of daily living – there can be an expectation that God will reveal himself as his people respond to their knowledge of him. Silence, prayer, meditation, praise, thanksgiving, confession and intercession all have a role to play in providing a context and backcloth for learning. In recent years the wind of liberation has blown through the worship life of many fellowships and God has been praised and worshipped afresh as he has spoken through word, prophecy and vision. Some have discovered new learning experiences in the context of this liberated worship. Others who do not share these experiences still need to see worship as a place where God speaks to the individual and to the church family as a whole. Learning devoid of worship and praise will be dry and hollow. Worship without learning and growth may be exciting but will remain shallow.

One-to-one: shepherd, counsellor, guide

We have placed a heavy emphasis on the church as a learning community, where people learn together. This has been a deliberate attempt to counteract an over-emphasis on the privatisation of learning. There were, however, times in Jesus's ministry when he took individuals aside to speak with them. In today's church we must not neglect the discipling that occurs between two people when one is helping the other. I would like to suggest three different situations in which this occurs:

Informal discussion
when Christian friends meet to discuss issues that face them, or to pray together. These are not structured meetings, but happen on odd occasions. Conversations may include the content of last week's sermon, a personal problem or sharing a happy occasion. Sometimes such contacts lead one or both of the parties further on in their discipleship. We can probably all recollect occasions that fit into this category.

Counselling/pastoral guidance
These occasions are a response to a need expressed by someone in the fellowship, a problem they wish to solve, or guilt, anxiety, or hurt they want to share, or a question they wish to have settled. In these situations individuals have a desire to move on in their lives, to change and grow, so counselling is a form of discipling. In this one-to-one situation one of the pair has some gift or training in counselling or pastoral methods and is recognised by others in the church as having this role. They may be part of a recognised pastoral team, consisting of, for example, the minister, an elder, deacon, home group leader, and professional counsellor (social worker, psychiatrist) who is a member of the church. But they should be people who have the relevant gifts or skills and not simply people with status or 'long-standing' in the church. These are people who are able to listen carefully to others and can help those who come to them to clarify their need and look for possible solutions. They are not quick to jump in with advice but may offer specific help when it is appropriate to do so. They are people able to confront those who are 'enjoying' their own problems, and also know when to refer difficult problems to others with more specialist skills.

Shepherding
This term has many different connotations for different sections of today's church. For some, it is a term almost synonymous with discipline. For our purposes I would like to introduce the idea as yet one more means by which

discipling can take place. There is a place for encouraging adults to find one other with whom they can meet for the specific purpose of finding encouragement and help in discipling. They may wish to call that person a 'mentor' or 'shepherd' or, to use Kenneth Leech's term, 'a soul friend'. The relationship between the two provides a foundation for sharing, a confidant perhaps, a sounding-board, an advisor. In churches where the word shepherding is in common use it is often closely associated with authority. I would suggest that there is value in developing such one-to-one discipling relationships *between equals* and possibly as *a mutual relationship*, perhaps between husband and wife or two friends of the same age and experience. These shepherding relationships may be as valuable as those between church 'elders' and their 'sheep'. The local church could encourage its members to take on this role, and help them to learn how to listen, ask questions and help others to reflect on their experiences.

Individual learning

Finally, we must mention growth through personal study and exploration, including personal Bible study, reading and video programmes used at home. As people face dilemmas in their discipling – questions of doctrine or problems in sorting out Christian attitudes to modern issues – they may need someone who can help them find the appropriate book or article; but more about this in chapter eight.

Helping Christians learn from everyday experiences

If we still have a lot to do in helping adults make the most of their learning in the teaching situations that already occur in and around our churches, we have to admit that we haven't even started to help adults cope with the incidental or informal learning that could result from everyday experiences. These events and activities have implications for each of us as disciples. In an attempt to grasp the range and scope of this dimension to discipleship some major themes are displayed in Figure 2.

Figure 2:	Potential growth points in everyday experiences
Personal growth and phases of life:	my identity and who I am my moods and feelings, and coping with them my inadequacy, lostness, aloneness my sexuality my marriage my family my career my retirement my usefulness
Crises:	career change redundancy marriage divorce moving home childbirth bereavement
Relationships:	coping with new relationships (spouse, children) coping with disagreement and conflict meeting others' needs and giving advice answering people's queries
Family:	being single bringing up children relationship with spouse relationship with parents and in-laws children leaving home
Social and political issues:	responding to the news coping with injustice around me voting taking responsibility in my community
Being a Christian:	at home at work at leisure with friends and relations

The issues listed are by no means complete; what is important is that they confront adults through everyday incidents at different times and in different ways. Some are sparked off by very minor activities like reading a newspaper, having a casual conversation on a bus or in a shop. Some occur through routine activities like getting the children ready for school. Some are concerned with major stages of life and are experienced over months or years – including the feelings of inadequacy some men feel during mid-life, the development of a relationship with a new spouse, or living through a depressive illness. Some may confront us as traumatic experiences, powerful and short-lived. These are all informal means of learning because they are not planned for the purpose of learning; despite this they may be important learning experiences – means by which God wants us to grow as disciples. The way people react and respond to these experiences is important for those who are concerned with adult discipleship. There are a whole range of reactions to informal learning experiences. The experience may: • raise a question in the individual's mind that is eventually answered, forgotten, or left unresolved; • create feelings of joy, fear, frustration, which are expressed, not understood, or hidden; • create problems that are solved, ignored or left open; • produce activity that is helpful or unhelpful, moral or immoral, uplifting or depressing.

Christian adults need to be helped to make sense of their experiences and to know how to grow from them in a positive way that will bring honour to God. But the learning potential of these experiences may diminish in direct proportion to the time that has elapsed since the experience occurred. In other words, the ideal time to help adults make sense and use of these experiences is soon after they have happened.

If we really want to help adults grow as disciples we must not ignore this vast learning resource. 'The classroom of life' is a term that contains much truth.

The local church can help in a number of ways:

1 Teach adults that they can learn and grow from their everyday experiences as well as through formal learning.

2 Use illustrations in talks and sermons that help make connections with people's real experiences.

3 Provide structures and opportunities for people to share and examine their experiences, and to come to expect others to help them make sense of experiences and to tackle major issues and problems. The house group may provide the best structure for this with times set aside for examining 'hot issues'.

4 Train the church as a whole in basic pastoral skills so that Christians can *listen* to others talking about their experiences and, instead of just giving advice, are able to use questions to help them think through what has happened to them.

5 See that those with suitable gifts in the church are trained in pastoral skills so that they can help people with particular problems ranging from crises (bereavement, marriage problems) to questions like, 'How can I answer my neighbour when she says. . ?'

6 Run specialist groups or short courses on relevant items in the list above, for example, three evenings on 'What do I do with my retirement?' A six-week parenthood course for those with children, an eight-week marriage enrichment course for those married five years or more, a day course on coping with unemployment.

7 Equip all Christians to tackle everyday issues as individuals or in the context of their households. One very important aspect of this involves helping people to handle the Bible properly for themselves, not just as an aid to devotions but as a tool to help them think and react in a Christian way to issues that face them.

8 Have books/resources on life-related topics easily available for people to borrow, including those from 'secular' publishers.

Keeping a record
Many adults like to make notes during teaching sessions and on occasions it is good to encourage this as it aids concentration and can prompt the memory for some time after the event. Teaching methods that encourage participation, however, make note-taking difficult. During informal experiences people do not usually stop to make notes for future reference, although some may keep diaries.

The learning diary provides a valuable means of personal record-keeping that enables individuals to keep notes of things experienced every day as well as during teaching sessions that involve a high degree of participation. When used during formal experiences participants have to be given time at various stages of the session to make notes. At the end of each section and at the end of the course participants can be encouraged to write down for their own record anything that has challenged them, annoyed them, introduced a new idea, mystified them, worried them, pleased them. In this way participants can record facts, feelings and questions that occur to them during open discussion, role play, simulation excercise, or after the showing of a film or slides. Some may even find it a help to have guidelines for their reflective record. The one illustrated in Figure 3, for example, has been used successfully on weekend conferences.

1 Things learned (feelings, questions, new ideas, etc.):	2 Possible consequences for me (of each item recorded in column 1):	3 Realistic action for me (as a result of each item recorded in column 1):

Some adults may gain from the discipline of keeping a regular, daily or weekly diary in which they record events in their lives. By sitting down regularly and reflecting on experiences, recording reactions and new insights, adults may be helped to make more sense of the incidental learning occurring every day and may be more able to discern God speaking to them in a variety of new ways.

Handling the Bible
Churches often work hard at providing a doctrinal base from which Christians can go out and live their lives, but each day we face issues that have no simple answers in the doctrinal teaching we receive. It may be good to be able to work *from* a solid understanding of biblical teaching *to* life situations but it is also essential that adults are able to work *from* life experiences back *to* the Bible to discover what God would teach them. How many churches actually train adults to use the Bible for themselves? This requires more than an encouragement to have some daily devotions, or pushing some Bible-reading scheme into their hands. It involves helping adults to interpret the Bible, knowing the importance of cultural context and the difference beween 'meaning' and 'application'. It involves helping people to trace teaching through scripture so that themes of particular relevance to them can be followed up with the help of a Greek Lexicon and an Analytical Concordance. It involves helping people to distinguish between different types of biblical writing and to know how to gain meaning from each. In helping people to learn from informal experiences we must give them tools as well as structures and the Bible, used in the right way, is an excellent implement.

The environment for discipling

Fixed pews, bare walls; comfortable seats, bright but 'safe' wallpaper; straight rows and seats in circles, all say something about discipling. If the surroundings are austere and formal people cannot be expected to relax and participate. But even in large group settings, seats that are moveable and reasonably comfortable can help to make a hall more conducive to learning. Arranging seats in a semi-circle rather than straight rows allows the participants to have some contact with each other as well as the speaker. Speakers who hide behind large tables, or stand at a great distance from the learners are saying something about the learning process. Walls that are decorated with warm colours, that are not littered with out-of-date posters but contain items to support the topic under consideration, all provide positive encouragement for learning. Small groups work better if seated in a circle where everyone can see everyone else, and address each other without the craning of necks. Even the temperature is important. Room temperatures need to be controllable to meet seasonal needs as well as the needs of different age groups. Ventilation should also be controlled so that people feel comfortable and able to work.

Exercises

1 What are the structures used for teaching in your church? Indicate how they are used against this check list:

- large group
- small group
- specialist group
- intergenerational group
- one-to-one
- individual learning

2 Think through your own life and list incidents and experiences that have been a source of learning and growth for you. How can you help members of your church or group to learn more from their informal experiences?

7   Training disciplers

7
Training disciplers

It is hard to find one word that describes the person who aids the adult in her growth as a disciple. A number of different words have been used in this book, most of which only describe one aspect of adult discipling. If a collective word is necessary then 'discipler' is as good as any other. The word 'teacher' is synonymous in the minds of many adults with the person who imparts knowledge – someone who, because of training, experience or special gifts, is able to tell others. Teachers are not, however, seen as people who can organise and run a participatory learning exercise or lead a small group or act as counsellor. In fact, many teachers are not able to cope with these aspects of discipling. On occasions we have used the term 'leader' – often when referring to small groups where someone takes responsibility for guiding the group rather than 'teaching' the group. But a leader only fulfils one element of the discipling process.

Categories of discipler

The word 'discipler' can be used to cover all aspects of adult discipling – teacher, group leader, enabler, speaker, specialist, counsellor, shepherd, friend. It includes people with special training and recognition, and those who help others informally – sometimes without knowing it themselves. It may be helpful to define four broad categories of discipler, each with a special function and each of which is needed in the local church. Some adult disciplers may have the experience, skills or gifts that fit them into more than one category; others may only be able to fulfil one function. The four categories are speaker, specialist, enabler, counsellor.

The speaker or orator

The speaker or orator is anyone with speaking gifts that enable them to teach or preach. They are able to address both large and small groups of people in such a way that their listeners retain interest and, through their listening, are encouraged to learn. A good speaker reaches people's emotions as well as their minds and has enough awareness of his listeners to make what he is saying relevant to their lives and needs. Jesus displayed these abilities; using vivid pictures and teaching relevant to the lives of his listeners. As well as being provocative, he attracted the crowds. The apostle Peter appears to have developed the same abilities, judging from his early performances recorded in the book of Acts.

The speaker usually has a message to communicate and has to tread a tight-rope, on one hand ensuring that his message is conveyed while on the other being sensitive to how his listeners are responding and ensuring that they are not left behind. The speaker who ignores his listeners and concentrates solely on his message may fail to communicate.

Speakers need to be able to order their material in ways that encourage people to follow their argument. This can be done by:

1 **having some chronological sequence:** as the Bible expositor who works systematically through a passage of scripture.

2 **developing the message from general principles to specific examples:** as the speaker who talks about the nature and function of the Holy Spirit before sharing his own experience.

3 **building up a picture by working from individual case studies or examples to generalisations and then back to the specific:** as the speaker who helps people make the application to their own lives. The missionary speaker, for example, may describe individuals from his work, use them to develop principles of mission, and then encourage listeners to respond with suggestions for how to evangelise as individuals or as a church.

4 stating a problem and then working through the solution or solutions: as the teacher who is trying to explore the relationship between evangelism and social concern.

5 comparing and contrasting two situations: for example, the exodus and the cross, as a means of understanding salvation.

Speakers also need to be able to present their material in an effective way by:

1 capturing their listeners' attention at the very beginning, during their first few sentences; then holding that interest and attention throughout by appealing to their curiosity, their emotions, their experience or by using vivid imagery, surprise, or immediate personal involvement.

2 using their voice to its best advantage by varying the tone, pitch, volume; and altering the pace at which they speak in order to hold attention, to emphasise points and communicate emotions.

3 using silence to emphasise what has been said or to give the listeners time to digest or to respond inwardly to the words.

4 using non-verbal communication to positive effect, especially facial expressions and the movement of hands and arms; but at the same time avoiding distracting non-verbal behaviour including mannerisms and excessive movement.

As well as using their gifts and skills the good speaker will be aware that the learner has a relatively passive role in this type of teaching situation and will, hopefully, look for ways of involving the learner – using some of the techniques described in chapter five.

The specialist
People with particular experience or knowledge that needs to be shared with others can be called 'specialist' teachers. They might include the theologian, archaeologist, overseas worker, social worker, psychiatrist, or solicitor; perhaps even someone who feels they have a message from God for a fellowship at a particular time. Many of the teachers in this category will have special understanding of, and insights into, the Bible or have specialist careers that can make some contribution to the growth of disciples in the local church. Specialists may be invited in to meet particular needs of a congregation in terms of knowledge, skills, sorting out problems or developing new practices. For example, a child psychologist may be invited to help Christian parents with their parenting problems, a married couple may be asked to speak at the marriage preparation course for engaged couples, a policeman may be invited to talk to a group of youth leaders, a relief worker may come to share something of his Third World experiences, a Christian psychiatrist may talk to the wives' group on 'Depression and the Christian' – the list is endless.

These people have something to teach but are not necessarily aware of how to communicate in a way that helps adult to learn. When we invite these people to make a contribution we should not be afraid to consult with them on their presentation, explaining the needs of their listeners and suggesting ways of encouraging participation in the session.

We often make a wrong assumption that because someone has something to share or to teach they will automatically have discipling skills. It is better to assume nothing! We can help by providing a structure for them in which to work in a way that will benefit the learners. The specialist may, however, be encouraged to improve her teaching skills and may find the skills described in a later section of this chapter a useful starting point.

The enabler

The major concern of the enabler or facilitator is to *create* learning situations. Such disciplers enable learning to take place and know how to structure situations so that adults, with all their fears and worries about learning and their individual needs, can grow. This role is of fundamental importance for the discipling of adults in the church today. It is people-oriented rather than message-oriented and although the *nature* of Christian discipleship is important to the enabler he is also concerned for the nature of the Christian's experience and the way this experience is used to promote growth into God's wholeness. An enabling dimension should and can be part of any teacher's role whether they be speaker or specialist but there is also a place for those who have specific enabling gifts and skills.

There are two levels at which an enabler can work in the local church to help the Christian disciple:

1 The 'director' has oversight of the teaching carried out through the local church as a whole. This role does not have to be assumed by the minister and in larger churches may be taken by another gifted teacher. The director is concerned for the variety of learning activities, the range of topics covered and the various structures in which learning takes place. The director attempts to see that the discipleship needs of the individual, group and total fellowship are met. These needs will be in the areas of understanding and knowledge of the Christian faith, skills for ministry, pastoral needs, Christian living etc. Acting as a co-ordinator, the director will have oversight of those responsible for the bookstall and resources area, as well as the teaching activities. As an enabler, he or she would make decisions in consultation with others in the church rather than being a lone executive.

2 Enablers may be the leaders of small groups: house groups, wives' groups, specialist groups, nurture groups, training courses. The enabler has responsibility for the learning of a group of adults with whom he or she would need to develop a relationship. She will be concerned to use all the resources and experience of the members of the group to enhance the discipling process. This type of teacher is a servant to the group, sensitive to the needs of the adult members and able to establish a climate where even the most reticent individual can unfreeze and grow.

The pastor/counsellor

Pastoring or counselling may not traditionally be seen as part of the discipling process. It has, however, the objective of moving Christians on in their lives, or helping them to get over some problem blocking their growth. A counsellor is similar to the enabler, but able to work with individuals rather than with groups. The skills a counsellor needs to develop include: being able to listen; helping people clarify their own problems and work at their own solutions; offering help and advice when and where appropriate.

In focusing attention on the skilled counsellor we should not neglect the shepherd and 'soul friend' who may not have specialist skills but who is still a discipler. Some fellowships may feel the need to establish or encourage a network of shepherds and may offer everyone adult training and teaching in fulfilling this discipling function.

Discipling skills

In describing the discipling process for adults in the church it may have become apparent that many more skills are required than are normally taught to those traditionally responsible for teaching adults. This is also true for secular adult education, although that is changing as evidenced in the Open University training packages for adult educators. The skills required will depend both on the type of discipling taking place and the size of the group involved. Some skills are more important for speakers and these have been described above. Others will be important for group leaders and some are important for anyone involved with adults. General skills include:

Personal awareness

Disciplers need to be self-aware. They should be conscious of their own gifts, skills and strengths and should also know their own weaknesses and limitations. Disciplers need to know what assumptions and presuppositions they bring to discipling. They may have particular attitudes and feelings about how teaching should take place.Their past experiences will have created expectations and biases which they may unwittingly communicate to other adults. These may on occasions act as a stumbling block to other adults. They should know how they respond to different teaching and learning situations – when there is conflict between people in groups, for example, or when emotions are expressed in a discussion, role play or experiential exercises. Finally, they should be growing themselves, looking for areas of their life and skills where they need to change and develop.

Sensitivity to other adults

Someone responsible for taking adults through a learning exercise should have some understanding of how adults feel. They should be able to discern the feelings of others in a group when they are expressed non-verbally rather than in words. Awareness of the fears and problems adults have when confronted with learning and change should induce a concern to see that obstacles are dealt with in a loving manner by whatever strategy is appropriate. This could include careful design of programmes; creating a secure climate by using particular teaching methods; gently confronting, counselling and supporting individuals; helping people to become aware of their feelings, etc. They need to be able to encourage adults as they learn, showing them that they are valued and that their growth is important for themselves and for God.

Ability to use different techniques
Disciplers need to know a range of techniques and how to use them so that people learn from their experiences. They need to know how to match techniques with the need and situation of those being discipled. They need to know how to introduce new techniques and how to encourage adults to participate without feeling insecure.

Ability to use resources
All disciplers need to know where to find, and how to use, resources; how to use material critically and to adapt it so that others can get the best from it. They should know how to handle the Bible themselves so that it becomes a potent tool in their own growth.

Design skills
These include the ability to consult with potential learners, set goals for a course or evening programme, arrange a programme that will maximise the learning of the adults attending, and knowledge of how to evaluate the event after it has occurred.

Enabling and counselling skills
These include:

1 The ability to listen to people as they talk or contribute, in an effort to hear and understand what they are saying, thinking and feeling.

2 The skill of communicating and enabling others to communicate, so that there is mutual understanding. This includes the ability to make what they are saying relevant and concrete for the listener and to check out whether others have understood them. It also includes ensuring that other people who contribute are understood and that difficult issues are clarified. Finally, it involves the ability to summarise a group's conclusions or discussions at the end of a session.

3 Coping with disagreement and conflict in a group, without getting so emotionally involved themselves that they become unable to help the parties to put their cases clearly. Ensuring that opposing sides understand each other fully and are encouraged to explore their differences and their feelings.

4 Being an encourager, providing positive support and affirmation to adults as they learn.

5 Boundary keeper – keeping the boundaries that the group has set in terms of time, task and personal responsibility, so that an element of discipline exists in the group.

6 Having the willingness to see those they are teaching develop the qualities and skills described above. In other words to be prepared to share their responsibilities as disciplers with the learners, some of whom may be potential disciplers themselves.

7 Having the ability to help others see their own problems and to work at solutions.

8 Having a knowledge of how a small group works, understanding the dynamics of the feelings, relationships and communication in a group.

9 Knowing how to handle different personalities and different roles that people take on in a group.

Creating a climate for learning

Disciplers of all types need to encourage disciples by creating a climate conducive to learning. This involves a number of skills:

- Discovering the needs of the fellowship or group.
- Producing, in consultation with others, a syllabus or plan of study.
- Choosing methods that encourage learning.
- Creating an atmosphere conducive to learning – secure, comfortable, honest, open.
- Helping the whole learning cycle to occur by being aware of the stages of learning.
- Helping the group and individuals to evaluate their learning experiences and to look for ways of building on or improving what has been accomplished in the past.
- Building relationships/friendships with individuals or groups so that a level of trust can be established.

The discipler as a model

Whether we admit to it or not, we all model ourselves on others to some extent. We have already considered how we are to model ourselves on Jesus, and Paul also tells his readers to model themselves on him. The teacher can also be a model for others in the church. Modelling is a means of informal learning, of which we may be completely unaware. It occurs when we take on the lifestyle, behaviour, attitudes, or even mannerisms of someone else. It can be a helpful and positive means of growth or it can be negative and inhibiting. On occasions disciplers may consciously model attitudes or modes of behaviour that they want learners to emulate. In a small group modelling can have a great impact. A leader may model open, non-judgemental attitudes to other adults in the group, the desire to listen to others, the willingness to share feelings as well as thoughts, encouragement of others, a desire to take learning and discipleship seriously, a willingness to participate and take risks, honesty and openness, and an acknowledgement that he/she is also open to learning. This may involve the leader in taking risks by saying and doing things that are not normally part of the group's experience. Taking risks like this may encourage others to do the same, accepting the leader's way of doing things as the norm. Modelling becomes unhelpful when it inhibits the development of natural strengths and skills in the learner or when it produces behaviour that is unconducive to the learner's growth. Because modelling often occurs without our knowledge, disciplers need to be aware of the process in the discipling situations for which they have some responsibility.

Training disciplers

Those who disciple others need training to be good teachers and leaders. There is no way we can satisfy those training needs in the pages of this book. That is the role of colleges, training organisations and, most important of all, the local church. We will limit our contribution to a list of topics that might be included in such teacher training. Hopefully there is no need to emphasise, at this stage of the book, that this training cannot be conducted simply through lectures – it must be conducted in the light of the learning cycle. There are three ways of training: ● on-the-job supervisory training – where new teachers and leaders are 'let loose' on the adults in the church but watched and supervised; ● 'classroom training' – where people are taken out of the real situation and trained on a course in the classroom; ● 'distance training' – where people are given a book, a programmed learning course or video and allowed to study on their own. In considering the training needed for different types of teaching the list in Figure 4 may be helpful.

All those with some responsibility for teaching adults will benefit from putting themselves in the place of learners. It is important to try to empathise with adult learners, whether through listening or being involved in experiential exercises, and so to understand some of the feelings of being a learner.

Figure 4: The skills of a discipler, and the means of acquiring them

SUBJECTS	METHOD OF TRAINING
Knowledge	
The discipler needs to know about:	
• the adult learning process	Talks; reflection on own experience.
• the Christian faith	Experiences of all sorts throughout one's Christian life.
• problems of adult learners	Talks; experience of adult learners; self-awareness; shared reflection on the past.
• the discipleship needs of adults	Surveys; questionnaires; case studies; chatting.
• the development of adults	Talks; case studies.
• his/her own presuppositions and experiences that may make it harder for others to learn	Small group discussion; values clarification exercises.
• resources	Displays; hand-outs.
Attitudes	
The discipler needs a:	
• desire to help others in their growth	
• concern to grow himself, both as a discipler and in areas of his own discipleship	Discussion; personal awareness exercises; talks; values clarification exercises.
• willingness to think critically about issues	
• concern for individuals	
Skills	
The discipler needs to have:	
• personal awareness of her own strengths, weaknesses, skills, needs	Experiential exercises.
• sensitivity to adults being taught: their feelings, problems, barriers in learning situations	Experience of group work; use of sensitivity training techniques.
• communication skills	Practical experiential exercises.
• pastoral skills: listening, clarifying, confronting and problem-solving	Role play; experiential exercises.

Skills – cont.

• use of a variety of teaching techniques, particularly those that encourage a high level of participation	Workshops; on-the-job training; talks.
• understanding of how to use the Bible	Practical exercises; case studies; discussion; talks.
• understanding of how small groups work	Small group training and on-the-job experiences.
• ability to design teaching programmes	Practical exercises; workshops.

Exercises

1 Who are the speakers, the specialists, the enablers, the pastors in your fellowship?

2 Below is a list of the skills mentioned earlier. Rate yourself against each one (1 = low in skill; 4 = high). Ask someone who knows you to do the same analysis. Then look at areas where you need to develop skills.

• Ability to listen to others	1 2 3 4
• Ability to communicate	1 2 3 4
• Ability to create a climate for learning	1 2 3 4
• Ability to cope with conflict	1 2 3 4
• Ability to use a variety of teaching materials	1 2 3 4
• Encourager of others as they learn	1 2 3 4
• Open minded	1 2 3 4
• Boundary keeper	1 2 3 4
• Desire to see gifts/skills developed in others	1 2 3 4
• Understanding other adults	1 2 3 4
• Knowledge of resources for adult discipling	1 2 3 4
• Ability to design teaching programmes	1 2 3 4

8 Tools for learning and teaching

that they need not condemn a whole book or article just because they disagree with some of the ideas and opinions, but can be selective in what is useful to them. One means of encouraging critical reading is to have regular reviews in both large and small teaching groups. This gives the reviewer the chance to model critical behaviour with statements like: '. . . don't accept it all!' 'I found one or two chapters difficult to accept.' 'If you feel confused by any of the arguments do chat them over with . . .'

or:

'This video is aimed at _____ (particular target group). If you don't qualify I would still recommend you see it, especially the second half which can apply to anyone.'

or:

'Remember as you read this article that it comes from one person's very special experience. It is not, necessarily, suggesting that you have the same experience but you may discover that the lessons learnt have some application to your own life.'

Using books, cassettes, videos, filmstrips and teaching programmes as resources in teaching sessions can also be a means of educating people in how to use these same resources themselves. Those who lead small groups, are involved in pastoring others, preach or give talks, may need help themselves in using resources and in how to encourage others to use resources critically.

Making resources available

Adults won't use material that is hard to get at and availability can take three forms:

Bookstall:
This should be stocked with books for sale which are clearly and attractively displayed in an accessible spot. A bookstall is an ideal means of providing individuals with discipling material. A good bookstall needs a good 'manager', someone who can keep the books up-to-date and relevant to the needs and wants of the congregation. The manager will need: • to encourage reading people to make their needs known; • to find ways of encouraging reading for personal growth in the fellowship as a whole; • to be aware of his or her own biases and interests and see to it that they do not influence the bookstall selection; • to keep abreast of new publications by taking one of the booksellers' magazines and, if possible, paying regular visits to local bookshops; • to encourage the reviewing of books that link with themes and issues being considered in some part of the fellowship, either through the church newsletter or magazine or more effectively through spoken review at meetings; • to help more people select books

appropriate to their needs in terms of age, depth and subject, and to encourage critical reading. In order to do this managers must be available to talk with and listen to those who enquire.

Libraries
Not everyone can afford to buy books and a church library provides learning resources for those who can't or won't spend money on books. Libraries, like bookstalls, need to be given a high profile if they are to be used effectively. The content of the library should be planned, so that it stocks books that will be helpful to people (rather than containing 'throw-aways' from those who have finished with particular books).

New books need to be added regularly to provide continuing interest. As with a bookstall the ideal would be to have someone responsible for the library who can see that the books meet needs expressed in the fellowship and amongst individuals. Books from the library can be reviewed, and reading encouraged, in the same way as through the bookstall.

Resource areas
Many teaching resources are often locked away in the minister's study, possibly a reflection of the old idea that the minister was the only teacher in the local church. Resource centres are areas where all resources are available for viewing and borrowing and are useful both to the teacher and the individual learner. The key to a good resource area is having everything carefully labelled, categorised and displayed or stored. In this way filmstrips, videos, maps and pictures as well as books, articles and journals can be located according to their subject matter. Someone wanting to prepare a house group study, talk, sermon, or do some personal exploration, can go to the appropriate shelf and find a variety of resources covering their topic. Resource areas may also stock material from missionary societies as well as current copies of Christian magazines and weekly denominational newspapers. If people are to be encouraged to browse and use the material on the spot the environment must be conducive to this with an easy chair as well as a table located nearby.

The users

In selecting resources for bookstall, library and resource area there are two categories of people to consider: the teacher/leader responsible for helping other adults in their learning, and the individual who wants to learn on his own.

Material for teachers could include: • Background preparation material: atlases; analytical concordances; word books; books on social, historical, geographical background; commentaries; dictionaries. • Teaching materials: adult teaching programmes; Bible study outlines; discussion starters;

filmstrips; soundstrips; audio cassettes; videos; 16 mm films. • Teaching aids: overhead projector; transparencies – homemade, and commercially produced; pictures; wall maps; charts. • Books on teaching adults: on the nature of adulthood; adult learning; teaching methods; communication skills; using audio-visual aids; counselling (including books mentioned in the further reading section of this book). The teacher will also require hardware in order to use the variety of audio-visual material already mentioned in chapter four.

The individual learner will have a greater range of needs: • Reference books: identical to the background preparation material mentioned above for those who teach. These also provide in-depth learning material for the individual. • Personal interests: books and pamphlets on issues that face the individual disciple in their everyday lives: to do with family life; bringing up children; lifestyle; social/political issues; doctrinal issues; or personal holiness. Where views on a particular topic are polarised, material covering the variety of views can help the adult to consider the issues critically. • In-depth study: some adults will want to follow-up some topics in depth and may require background books that probe beneath the surface. In addition to books, journals and periodicals will also be helpful here. • Follow-up material: material that allows individuals to follow up teaching programmes or sermons.

In selecting resource material or recommending study material to teachers and learners it is important to remember that there may be valuable insights contained in 'secular' books and audio-visuals produced by educational establishments and organisations. Critical examination remains an important tool in taking and applying this material to Christian discipleship.

Learning elsewhere

The Christian is not restricted to the guided discipling that he receives through the local church, and a much forgotten source of Christian education for the adult is provided by outside agencies. It may be difficult for members of a fellowship to gain access to the necessary information as many of the brochures advertising such courses end up in a minister's bin. One way to overcome this would be to have a notice board devoted to 'outside' events. Members of the congregation wanting to develop their understanding or skills in some area may find their needs met at a summer school, a weekend conference, training course or evening seminar. In raising the Christian's awareness of the availability of such courses we must not neglect those organised by secular groups – local authority evening classes, courses put on by voluntary organisations with a role in the community, counselling courses etc.

The following groups could be contacted with respect to courses and conferences: ● Bible and Theological Colleges (evening, weekend, and correspondence courses; summer school). ● Missionary Organisations. ● Denominational organisations (at national and local level). ● Non-denominational organisations and training agencies. ● Open University (which runs short courses as well as degree courses). ● Local Education Authorities (evening classes). ● Community Colleges (where they exist, they may have adult courses).

Where course fees are high churches may wish to subsidise those they would like to attend such courses.

Courses may well be run by those with little knowledge of the different ways in which adults learn. They may not know how to help those attending apply the course to their own lives and work back in their own fellowships. Those who are despatched to courses can be asked to report back to elders, house groups, leadership teams, or pastors who will not only receive the report but encourage the participant to consider how the learning can be applied 'back home'.

Computers

We end this chapter as we began, with computers. In some instances computers have replaced the teacher, so providing a further resource for the adult learner. As a teaching tool they are ideal for individual learning and are excellent for passing on facts and information as well as helping people to develop problem-solving and decision-making skills (useful for the Church Council!).

Where self-testing and checking is built into a computer programme it is called programmed learning. Those adults motivated to continue their learning at home may be able to obtain programmed-learning kits that enable them to learn New Testament Greek, Old and New Testament Studies, Church History and so on. Such programmes are not, as yet, available to buy, although this could change in the near future. There may, however, be someone in your church able to write the programmes for you. A whole course on Christian basics could be provided for individual learning at home. Its advantage is that it can enable fact-based individual learning for those who have a high degree of motivation (and who know which keys to press!). The big disadvantage is that the computer is a passive learning tool and involves limited use of the senses. This is a limitation that needs to be taken seriously in the light of the rest of this book.

Computers have one other function which could be of use to the learning resources of any local fellowship, and that is their ability to store information. Using a database programme, information can be stored under a variety of categories and retrieved at the press of a button. With the variety of educational information available in the form of books, audio-visuals, and organisations some churches may see value in being able to obtain a computer print-out of all resources available to the church on any given topic – counselling, Bible reading, Christianity and the nuclear arms race, suffering and so on. If someone has the time to put all the information on the computer and to keep it up to date this form of storage and retrieval can save much time and effort.

Exercise
Review the resources available in your church.
Consider ways of improving them and making them more available.

9 Designing learning programmes for adults

9
Designing learning programmes for adults

The word curriculum is, to some, synonymous with the packaged learning materials bought from a publisher, usually in printed form. In its broadest sense, however, 'curriculum' simply refers to a plan or strategy for learning and growth. In our context, its object is to give direction to the teaching and learning in the local church – a direction which should bear some relationship to the needs of those who experience it. In this last respect home-made curricula are the most effective in the local church because they have the potential for being the most relevant. Published resources have to be treated selectively and adapted to ensure they fit church needs.

Diagram 6:   Designing a church learning programme

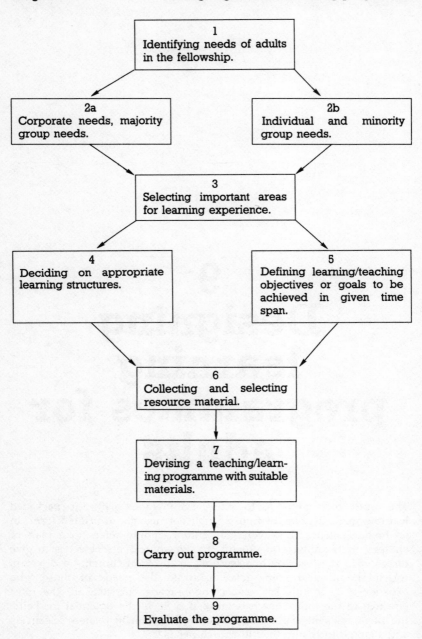

128

Often adult teaching schemes used in churches take no account of the diversity of adults in the fellowship – new and old Christians, married and single, academic and non-academic – as well as all the important discipleship issues relevant to minority groups (such as training for an area of ministry, handling particular stages in life, counselling needs).

One answer to this is to provide some common core teaching covering major themes relevant to the church as a whole and around this to build specialist and optional learning sessions.

1 Identifying needs

It is important that, in identifying needs, those who are to be on the receiving end of a teaching programme have an opportunity to contribute to the content and planning of that programme. Adults are aware, to some extent, of their own needs and should be encouraged to air them. If people are involved from the outset there is a greater likelihood that they will be committed to any programmes or plans made for them. Collecting this information is obviously time consuming but it can be streamlined by issuing people with questionnaires to fill in or by setting up an *ad hoc* planning group made up of representatives from interested parties (church eldership, leaders or teachers, and those on the receiving end).

Needs should also be identified by someone or some group within the fellowship, who has spiritual insight into the church's discipleship needs. This may be the function of an eldership group, the church pastoral team, the church education group, a group of deacons, the ministers or the church council. In New Testament times the person or group involved in this process was recognised as having some spiritual oversight in the fellowship and the ability to discern needs.

This group has to be *particularly* sensitive to their own biases, hobby-horses and interests and any presuppositions they may bring to their understanding of discipleship. This creates a twofold way of identifying needs, and to use one way without the other has the danger of producing a programme that only meets half the discipleship needs of the adult fellowship.

In order to prevent the planning group from becoming too narrow in their identification of needs, a wide range of potential areas of need could be listed including: doctrinal; problem-centred; systematic; life-centred; practical skills; personal, corporate and immediate 'hot' issues; needs related to attitudes and values; emotional and psychological development; behaviour; lifestyle; knowledge and understanding.

2a Corporate needs

At any time in the life of the church there will be needs that affect the church as a whole. Here, teaching and learning strategies have to be developed for the church as a whole. These may include teaching on doctrinal issues, the tackling of practical problems that face the whole congregation, teaching and training as preparation for a church that is commencing on a major project, or teaching to correct some imbalance that has crept into church life.

2b Individual and minority group needs

There will be many more issues that only affect groups and individuals within the fellowship. These will include, for example, training in leadership skills for those in specific areas of ministry; help for those going through particular phases or stages in their lives; specialist doctrinal teaching for new Christians, or those wanting to look in depth at particular areas of Christian belief; membership instruction; those with particular pastoral needs.

3 Selecting priorities

From the information collected at stages one and two there must now be some selection of priorities, which items to tackle first, and how long to spend on them. Again, there will be greater commitment from the total fellowship if they have some influence in this process. However, the final selection of priorities may result in frustration for some whose needs cannot be catered for. In such cases the individuals concerned should be encouraged to explore the issues omitted, through personal study, shepherding or the formation of informal groups. The church as a whole may find it helpful to have 'report-back' sessions from such smaller groups.

4 Deciding on appropriate learning structures

In chapter six we looked at some of the different structures for learning. Some of the learning priorities identified in stage three may very obviously fit better into one structure than another. However, it is important when deciding on suitable structures, to bear in mind the considerations outlined in our first three chapters. Hopefully, the church will use all the structures available to it. Through this variety – large group, small group, specialist group, intergenerational activity, pastoral and individual systems – it should be possible to meet the discipling needs of each member.

Issues concerning the whole church may initially be tackled in the large group setting and followed up in more depth through multiple small groups.

Minority topics and skills training, or issues that involve people's problems or facing personal issues, require the small or specialist group.

Individual needs may be met through stocking the bookstall or church library with books and audio-visual material on the necessary topics.

If pastoral care is to continue to be a valid means of discipling then the members of the pastoral team will need their thinking and skills sharpened regularly. This is especially important when particular problems gain a high profile in the church, such as the sudden death of a respected figure in the church creating anxiety and questions over healing and death. One means of ensuring that important issues are dealt with effectively is to integrate teaching topics into a combination of different groups. For example, a topic is first considered in the large group through a sermon or talk, then worked at in more detail in the small group, with individual learning materials (books etc.) available on the same topic for those wanting to do their own personal study. Such integrated programmes may vary in length from one week to a whole term, but seem to have most impact when they are of short duration (three–five weeks). They are a means of encouraging exploration and learning at different levels and in different ways, and enabling adults with different abilities, experience and styles of learning to benefit.

One particular type of integrated programme is the 'project'. This is limited in its duration and focuses on a topic with some immediate practical relevance. The project may involve using different sizes of groups and combine study and action as well as all the generations in the church. Three examples of integrated programmes are included below.

INTEGRATED PROGRAMME: EXAMPLE 1
Theme: Four-week teaching course on evangelism

Sermons on three consecutive Sundays providing inspirational teaching to the whole church.

Parallel work in house groups (or in small groups at three mid-week meetings) working at practical skills of sharing faith with friends.

Practical project in week 3 – evangelistic church meeting, neighbourhood door-to-door visiting, supper parties, coffee mornings etc.

Worship, prayer and evaluation in week 4 to provide the final part of the project. In small and/or large group.

INTEGRATED PROGRAMME: EXAMPLE 2
Theme: Two-week series on needs in the Third World

Two Sunday services with special focus on the Third World, with guest speakers. Sunday afternoon simulation game.

Saturday afternoon intergenerational project with whole church involved; followed by tea.

Bookstall focus on Third World issues.

Mid-week meeting or house groups exploring personal and corporate responses to Third World problems.

INTEGRATED PROGRAMME: EXAMPLE 3
Theme: Four-week exploration on the Bible

Family service/intergenerational activity introducing the theme to whole church.

Choice of training sessions–series lasting four evenings spread over four weeks on theme of 'How to use the Bible':
1 for beginners
2 for home group leaders
3 for those looking for new approaches to Bible study

A display in the church hall or entrance area exploring origins of the scriptures, and methods of Bible reading.

Bookstall of aids to Bible reading and books on the Bible, with reviews given at main meetings.

In this last example the addition of optional teaching groups helps to provide for the wide variety of needs and experience in the fellowship.

5 Defining learning goals

The-well worn adage, 'If you know what you're aiming at you're more likely to hit it', contains an element of truth when it comes to planning discipling programmes. Having consulted those taking part in the programme, to gain an understanding of their needs, planners can now ask themselves, 'What do we hope will be achieved through this programme?' There is a great deal of value in actually writing these learning goals down and even sharing them with those taking part right at the start of the teaching. Again let's look at some examples.

DEFINING LEARNING GOALS: EXAMPLE 1
Theme: A series of studies for small groups on suffering.

During these studies on suffering we hope that:
1 Individuals will gain a greater understanding of the nature and causes of suffering as seen through the eyes of Job and Jesus.
2 There will be an opportunity to share our own experiences of suffering and how we have responded to those experiences.
3 The groups will discover how they can better help members who at any time experience real suffering.
4 Those with pastoral gifts will become more sensitive to the needs of those who suffer.

DEFINING LEARNING GOALS: EXAMPLE 2
Theme: Day 'get-together' for house group leaders

The objectives of this day are:
1 To provide leaders with an opportunity to share particular problems faced during the past year in the areas of:
• content (studies undertaken)
• group (keeping the group alive)
• individuals (meeting individual members' needs)
• leadership (other issues concerned with being a leader).

2 To develop skills in preparing a Bible study from scratch – without using packaged programmes.
3 To develop skills in handling difficult group members in a discussion and to be sensitive to the cause of their behaviour, eg. the over-talkative and the withdrawn members.
4 To plan an outline for the next session of Bible studies.

DEFINING LEARNING GOALS: EXAMPLE 3
Theme: Sermon series on 'Discipleship as seen in Luke's Gospel'.

1 To broaden understanding of the nature of discipleship and to see how it influences the whole of life's activities.

2 To challenge people to:
* look at areas of their own lives where they need to grow and change;
* decide how those changes can come about.

3 To develop an attitude of openness to continuing growth and change.

4 To encourage Christians to face up to the suffering involved in being a disciple and to help them to discover practical ways in which they can find support during difficult times.

5 To challenge Christians to face up to the servanthood nature of discipleship and to encourage the practical outworking of this at home, work and in the church family.

When setting goals it may be helpful to distinguish between four broad categories:

Understanding/knowledge: the facts/knowledge/insights that you want people to have as a result of the discipling (eg. goal 1 of the Discipleship series).

Attitudes or values: a deeper, more fundamental influence over, or change in, people's attitudes, that will affect the way they look at and react to things in the future (e.g. goal 4 of the studies on suffering and goal 3 of the Discipleship series).

Skills: the development of practical skills that improve an individual's ability to perform a task or fulfil a role (eg. goal 3 of the studies on suffering, goals 2 and 3 of the house group leaders' day).

Action/behaviour: actions or changes in behaviour that, hopefully, will result from the learning experience (eg. goal 2 for the studies on suffering, goal 5 of the Discipleship series).

It is the last of these categories which is most often neglected; yet it is this one which completes the learning cycle, as described in chapter three.

The setting and declaring of discipling goals fulfils an important function in helping adult disciples, but it is not without its dangers. The greatest danger is that goal setting actually *limits* the learning that takes place through a course or event. Those taking part become blinkered by what they are supposed to learn, and serendipitous learning is suppressed. It may also be wondered whether it prevents God's Spirit from leading people in unplanned-for and unexpected ways. The session speaker or teacher may also be blinkered by pre-set goals and may develop an insensitivity to unplanned learning, discouraging people who, legitimately, want to follow new lines of discovery.

If these dangers are to be avoided it is important to recognise that learning cannot be totally planned for and that even in the most formal and structured setting different participants will be learning different things. The more informal and unstructured the 'teaching' the greater will be the diversity of actual learning taking place in those present. Goals simply represent a response to the needs discovered earlier in the planning phase and they exist as *potential* outcomes of teaching/learning sessions.

If goals are seen by teacher and learner more as guidelines or points of reference than compulsory outcomes then we are more likely to guard against being shackled to them.

The advantages of having stated goals outweigh the dangers. Primarily they show that there is a purpose in meeting together and that this purpose relates to the expressed and perceived needs of the people attending. They suggest that meeting together will result in some change (in knowledge/ understanding, attitudes, skills, behaviour or action), and help to reinforce an understanding that discipling implies change. Finally, they provide some yardstick by which 'growth' can be measured – useful to both the participant and the leader/teacher/organiser.   In small groups it may be appropriate to allow the whole group to participate in setting goals. Before the group sets out on its chosen topic or project, individuals can be asked to write down and share what they would hope to gain for themselves from their time in the group (expectations, fulfilment of personal needs) and what they would hope the group as a whole would gain (corporate learning and growth).

In large groups this participative goal setting and sharing becomes more impractical although each person attending could be asked to think about their own expectations and communicate them with one other person as a means of clarifying their own thoughts.

6 Collecting Resources

The vast amount of teaching/learning resource material in the form of books, audio-visuals, and teaching packages can be both a curse and a blessing to anyone trying to plan a teaching session. Choosing from the range may seem like a nightmare especially when no single item really meets your particular requirements. One common reaction to this is to give up looking, to ignore material created elsewhere and to produce your own. This has the advantage of ensuring that the material fits your situation. But it has the disadvantages of taking a vast amount of time and creative energy and being limited in its scope and content by your own experience and expertise. So the time you take in searching through shelves of resources in the local Christian bookshop may eventually save you time and effort. The use of other resources, channels, experience, expertise, knowledge and skills from outside the fellowship can add to the richness of the learning that takes place.

When collecting materials for a particular event there is a wide variety of possibilities:

1 Background material – material for a leader or teacher to help in the leading or teaching. These could include commentaries, fact sheets, dictionaries, articles, informal chats with others who have specialist knowledge or experience, studying other teaching programmes.

2 Aids for the learners to use – everything mentioned above plus audio-visual aids, maps, questionnaires, handbooks, sets of questions, pictures, visits, teaching programmes. Whatever the resource material used, it should help meet the goals that have been set for the course and not become an obstacle. Many an adult study group has set out with enthusiasm to tackle an area of concern or interest, only to find their energy diverted into trying to understand the meaning of the questions set by the minister or arguing over why the teaching programme isn't theologically accurate!

Those responsible for leading groups need to view all the resources they use critically and must be prepared to adapt them to fit in to what they want for their group. Here are some questions you could ask when considering how to use resource material prepared by someone else:

1 Which parts need to be selected to cover the learning needs defined for this group and to help achieve these goals?

2 How much of this material can be used in the time available to the group?

3 How should the material be altered to fit the needs of adult learners? Are questions worded in the most helpful way? Do examples need to be changed to fit the experience of the learners? What help is given to encourage the application of learning to living?

4 What needs to be added to the material to make it a useful tool for our purposes?

The ability to adapt resource material is a skill that will develop with time. Those who are new to it may struggle at first and will need guidance from those more experienced. Those with more experience are usually able to alter material to their own and their recipients' needs reasonably quickly.

7 Devising a programme/selecting techniques

Techniques play an important part in encouraging the discipling process and need to be selected with care. When used sensitively they can make all the difference between more information crammed into a tired brain and a new approach to living.

In selecting techniques remember:

1 Variety is important as a means of keeping interest and catering for the variety of people present.

2 Pace the programme so that it isn't too full. Use techniques that encourage reflection so that participants can absorb and apply experiences.

3 Use methods that maximise participation so that communication isn't one way – from teacher to learner.

4 Use methods, and structure the time, to enable people to respond emotionally to the programme – so that they know how others feel as well as what they think.

5 Use techniques that encourage the process described by the learning cycle: experience ---> reflection ---> conceptualising ---> application/action/practice.

The techniques chosen need to be appropriate to the learning that is required. The technique should act as slave to the learning, not vice versa – like the speaker who finds an excellent visual aid and then tries to work out what to teach using it, or the small group leader who stumbles across a magnificent simulation game and tries to squeeze it into a study programme for which it is inappropriate. Some learning situations are best serviced by particular techniques. One of the skills of the adult discipler is to find and use what is appropriate. The diagram below provides one means of categorising learning techniques which may aid the discipler. The horizontal scale describes the amount of control in the hands of teacher and learner and the vertical scale the level of participation (passive involving limited use of senses, active involving a variety of senses).

Sample methods have been marked on Diagram 7 to give some idea of where they fit against the two scales. There has been no attempt to place each technique in relation to all the others.

Diagram 7: Learning techniques, showing amount of leader control and learner participation

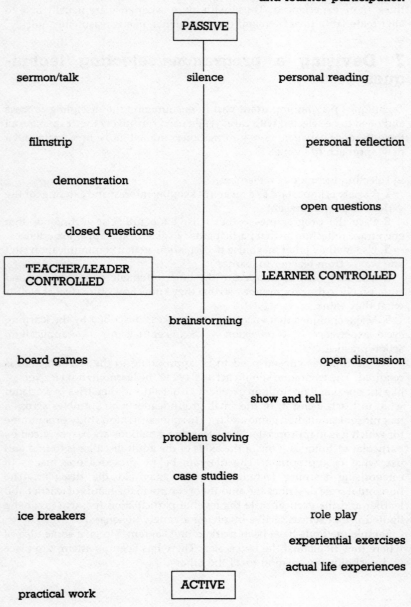

PASSIVE

sermon/talk   silence   personal reading

filmstrip   personal reflection

demonstration

open questions

closed questions

TEACHER/LEADER CONTROLLED   LEARNER CONTROLLED

brainstorming

board games   open discussion

show and tell

problem solving

case studies

ice breakers   role play

experiential exercises

actual life experiences

ACTIVE

practical work

Techniques with a high element of activity take longer but often have more lasting impact. Techniques that enable more control from the learner are risky from the point of view of the teacher who wants to encourage learning in specific areas, but they may promote greater commitment to change from the learner and may bring a richer variety of unexpected resources to aid the learning. Each technique has a place in the adult's learning programme and some are more obviously suited to particular occasions.

For example:

• Passive, teacher-controlled techniques are suited to teaching that requires real specialist knowledge and involves large crowds. • Learner-controlled techniques are suited to individuals or groups who are highly motivated or who need to be motivated to learn. • Active teacher-controlled techniques are ideal for training people in skills – the pastoral team or Bible study leaders. • Active methods are ideal for encouraging application and change through learning, and help people discover the emotional dimension to their discipleship.

In addition to knowing which technique to choose, a leader needs to know how to use a variety of methods, and needs to be sensitive to the effect the technique has on those taking part. He must be flexible enough to change the technique if necessary, in order to maximise the learning experience for those participating.

8 The Programme

The culmination of all the analysis, fact-finding and planning is a teaching programme that will provide people with the stimulus to learn. There will be an opportunity for participants to reflect on the experience – silently, through discussion and questions guided by the teacher, or time to work it out for themselves, individually. Participants are then encouraged in some way or other to see how this fits in with their existing knowledge – does it pose new questions? Challenge old ideas? How can it become part of me?

Finally, the programme will encourage participants to *use* their learning. The link may involve the disciples in verbalising what they might do as a result of the learning. Alternatively the fellowship may be able to offer opportunities • for the new learning to be 'lived out' as in the evangelistic project, • for group commitment to a changed lifestyle, • to serve the church fellowship in some way.

A teaching programme isn't complete unless the opportunity and encouragement to live out the learning is incorporated.

9 Evaluating the programme

For many, the completion of a teaching programme marks the end of all the planning and preparations and the time to begin to think about the next programme. If this is the case then evaluation is neglected and the adult teacher may miss out on an important learning experience for herself.

Evaluation is in part a reflective process, looking back over what has occurred and making sense of the experience. It is a means of exploring the effectiveness of a discipling course and discerning whether growth is really taking place in the lives of disciples and in the life of the church family. It is a way of ensuring that the church's discipling programme itself changes and grows, becoming more relevant and effective and hence glorifying to God.

The starting place for evaluating a programme is with the goals set in the beginning. The evaluator must go back to the changes in knowledge/attitude, skills, action and behaviour that the programme hoped to achieve. He may want to add to these any new or modified goals that were identified as the programme progressed.

The next task is to discover how well these goals have actually been achieved. This information can be collected in a number of different ways:

1 Personal discernment, where the teacher uses his/her own feelings, insights, observations and conversations to judge effectiveness. Where changes are evident in people's lives, and positive comments are made about the value of the programme, there is evidence that the programme has achieved something for the adults involved.

2 Individual structured evaluation, asking participants to talk about what *they* have learned and how *they* have changed as a result of the programme. It may be appropriate to remind them of the learning goals and to encourage them to assess the programme in relation to these.

There should be some opportunity during this type of evaluation for participants to share their emotional response to the programme. Did they feel safe to explore new areas? Did they feel threatened, frustrated, angry? Did they feel encouraged, supported? All this information can be collected through discussion or by asking people to fill in a questionnaire (a sample questionnaire is reproduced below).

3 Questionnaire: where the programme has been conducted in small groups the whole group may want to spend time looking back at its usefulness to them as a group as well as to individual members.

Figure 5:   Sample evaluation questionnaire

Course _____ .

Please help us design a better teaching programme in the future by answering these questions and returning the form to ....

Content
1 Did you find the course useful for your own Christian life? Yes/No

2 What did you find particularly helpful?

3 If you found anything unhelpful or puzzling please explain what.

4 Which of the goals set out at the beginning of the session do you feel were achieved for you?

5 How do you think you will be able to use this course in your own life?

6 Were there lessons on this course for our church/group as a whole?

7 Were there topics left out that you feel should have been covered?

Timing
8 Was the course (please ring any that are appropriate):
at the right time
at a bad time
too short
too long
just right?

9 How could timing have been improved for you?

Design
10 Did the course help you to learn new things? If 'no', say what made it difficult. If 'yes', say what helped.

11 What were your feelings as the course progressed (eg. apprehensive, excited, bored)?

12 Any other comments . . . ?

The evaluation will be looking for the answer to a number of questions:
- Did we get it right – did we identify needs correctly, set the right goals?
- Did we explore the issues in the right type of group? Was a small group, large group or whatever the best way?
- Did we have enough resources and were they the right ones?
- Did we use the right methods?
- Did we handle the problems that arose on the course effectively?

The result of the evaluation will depend on the findings but may involve:
- The complete re-design of a course for future use.
- The decision to repeat the course in the same way at another time.
- The identification of skills lacking in the teacher.
- The identification of new learning needs of disciples.
- The further adaptation of resources used.
- The decision to work harder next time at using a particular technique.

Exercises

1 Use the flow chart at the beginning of this chapter to analyse your present teaching programmes (sermon series, wives' group programme, house group series, training scheme, confirmation/membership class).

2 Produce a sample programme for one group in your church using the flow chart as your planning guide.

3 Produce a four-week integrated programme on a theme or Bible passage, using the flow chart as a planning guide.

4 Devise learning schemes for the different age groups in your church, based on your understanding of their needs and on the chart (ch. 3) describing the phases of adult development. As a guide, use the following age groups: 18–30, 30–40, 40–50, 50–60, 60+.

10   Encouraging change in the church

10
Encouraging change in the church

Learning involves change. Developing new approaches to learning and teaching in the church requires change: change in emphasis and approach, change even in structures and programmes. It may be difficult to encourage change in individual Christians but attempting to make changes in a church, made up of so many groups and sub-groups, is fraught with even more problems.

Before deciding to make changes we must first be convinced that they are going to improve our discipling of adults and so glorify God. Changes *must* therefore be carried out in the context of prayer; it is essential before, during and after implementing change.

Having discerned that change is appropriate we must recognise potential resistance and realise that change can be made more acceptable when carried out in the context of consultation and discussion with those who will be affected. The process should involve communicating the rationale behind the change and seeking reactions to it. There is something to be said for preparing the fellowship for a new move.

Sometimes change occurs in dramatic ways, with far-reaching effects right from the start. There are many instances where God's Spirit has swept through a local church in this way. But often change is more gradual and has to be helped along. This may mean that instead of developing completely new systems for discipling in the church it may be more effective, in the long run, to start with practices and structures that already exist and to adapt and develop these before introducing more radical changes. There are two questions that churches often neglect to ask themselves before embarking on a programme of change: • 'What do we hope to achieve by making changes?' and • 'How will we know we've achieved anything as a result of the changes?'

This book has invited you to look again at the way you disciple adults in your church, the way *you teach* and the way *they learn*. It has placed great emphasis on adult participation in the learning process and given a broad picture of how and when learning takes place. Using this framework, you may want to encourage more effective discipling, learning and change.

You may want adults to be more open to God's voice as his Spirit speaks through a wide variety of people and events.

The evidence that these purposes have been achieved will be in the growth seen in individual and fellowship life.

Areas of change

There are five broad categories that require changing if all that has been written about adult discipling is to be taken seriously and applied. These are changes in:

> Knowledge and understanding
> Attitudes
> Methods
> Skills and roles
> Structures

Each of the following four Figures takes one broad area of church teaching and examines it to see how each of the five categories listed above may be affected (these are all hypothetical situations).

Figure 6:   Changes to be made in sermon/talk content
                                            and style

Area of change	Changes
KNOWLEDGE AND UNDER-STANDING	1 Awareness of the value and limitations of the sermon as a means of helping adults learn about their faith. 2 Awareness of the range of techniques that could make the sermon a more effective teaching tool.
ATTITUDES	1 Ministers need to see the sermon as only one means of helping adults learn about their faith. 2 Ministers need to put more value on other teaching/learning methods. 3 Learners may also need to accept other teaching methods alongside the sermon.
METHODS	1 Speakers and teachers should make more use of symbolism and analogy in their sermons. 2 Speakers should apply the learning cycle to sermons, and so place more emphasis on application.
SKILLS	1 Speakers and teachers should improve their communication skills by developing the use of voice and body in talks.
STRUCTURES	1 Sermon time is to be shortened and time given for talk-back and discussion in small groups.

Figure 7:   Changes to be made in house group system

Area of change	Changes
KNOWLEDGE AND UNDER-STANDING	1 A new understanding of the role and purpose of house groups is to be communicated to everyone. 2 The function of an enabling leader is to be explained to leaders. 3 Leaders are to be taught about the workings of small groups. 4 Better knowledge of the Bible is to be encouraged in leaders.
ATTITUDES	1 Group members will be encouraged to value peer group learning. 2 Group members will be helped to see the need for participation. 3 Leaders are to be shown the importance of application in learning. 4 Everyone is to be encouraged to recognise the importance of relationships in groups.
METHODS	1 Use of a greater variety of methods. 2 Introduction of participatory learning methods into group. 3 Use of leadership skills that enable learning.
SKILLS	1 Leaders have to acquire/develop enabling, communication and pastoral skills.
STRUCTURES	1 Introduction of house groups to church. 2 Decisions have to be made on the regularity of group meetings.

Figure 8:   Changes to be made in teaching programmes
used in small groups

Area of change	Changes
KNOWLEDGE AND UNDER-STANDING	1 Leaders must be helped to see the variety of subjects relevant to adult disciples. 2 Leaders must understand the current discipleship issues that face the adults in the church/group.
ATTITUDES	1 Encourage everyone to see the importance of facing hot issues in home groups. 2 Encourage leaders to see the value of evaluating the programmes used. 3 Encourage leaders to see the importance of developing programmes that lay stress on application and action.
METHODS	1 Give leaders a new framework to help them plan programmes. 2 Introduce a regular meeting so that there can be some shared planning.
SKILLS AND ROLES	1 Train leaders in how to plan a programme. 2 Train leaders in how to evaluate a programme.

Figure 9: Changes to be made in total adult teaching/
learning approach in the church

Area of change	Changes
KNOWLEDGE AND UNDER-STANDING	1 Improve knowledge of how learning in adults take place. 2 Improve understanding of Christian faith and the nature of discipleship.
ATTITUDES	1 Help teachers and leaders to see that there is value in peer learning. 2 Help everyone to see that teaching is more than imparting knowledge, but involves the emotions as well. 3 Help everyone to see that discipleship is a process involving continuous learning and growth and is not static.
METHODS	1 Introduce new participatory teaching methods – role play, experiential exercises, ice-breakers. 2 Encourage the preparation of relevant programmes. 3 Introduce methods of evaluating the effectiveness of a programme.
SKILLS	1 Introduce new enabling skills: creating the right climate for learning. 2 Train group leaders in the use of participatory methods. 3 Train gifted people in counselling skills: listening, clarifying, enabling.
STRUCTURES	1 Introduce specialist teaching groups providing a choice of learning for adults in the church. 2 Introduce house groups. 3 Change nature of mid-week church meeting.

The hardest area to change is that of attitude. New methods may be introduced, new skills developed in those responsible for teaching and leading, new types of meeting may even have been introduced, but all this may be thwarted by fundamentally unaltered attitudes to adulthood, the learning/teaching process, or the nature of discipleship. Attitudes have their foundation in childhood and are reinforced through the experiences of adolescence and the early adult years – so they are not easy to change. Where it is important to change attitudes we must treat the task as both a spiritual and educational one. This involves seeking God's help through his Spirit, as well as teaching about the changes, modelling the changes and giving people the opportunity to experience them (in gentle, safe ways). We also need to recognise that some will never accept change and may eventually move on or may be deeply upset by change and need individual care and support.

A strategy for change

1 Improve the learning potential in the things you already do.
2 Consider neglected areas that can be incorporated into what you already do.
3 Change activities that need a radical shift of emphasis.
4 Introduce new activities that need to be introduced.
5 Prepare people for change – teaching, training, consultation, prayer. (Persevere, don't give up when faced with resistance. Be sensitive, and counsel. Take people through change slowly and explain why things are being done. Support and encourage; challenge and confront.)

Exercises

To help you change:

1 List the items from this book that are important for you and need to become part of your church's understanding and practice in discipling adults. For each item on the list note the changes that will be necessary under the headings: Knowledge/understanding, Attitudes, Methods, Skills and roles, and Structures.
2 Use the questionnaire below to pinpoint areas of change.

Ring the figure that reflects your situation: 1 = none or poor; 4 = a great deal or very good

1 How much specific help is given in sermons and groups to help adults apply teaching to their actual lives?　　　　1 2 3 4

2 How much opportunity in sermons is there for questions and come-back?　　　　1 2 3 4

3 How much use is made of aids (visual and other) during sermons and talks?　　　　1 2 3 4

4 What opportunity is given for the use of teaching methods other than talks?　　　　1 2 3 4

5 What opportunity and encouragement is given for people to explain and explore issues, crises, etc. that they have in their own lives?　　　　1 2 3 4

6 What involvement do the adults have in planning teaching courses?　　　　1 2 3 4

7 How much emphasis is placed on the individual needs of adults by providing a variety of learning opportunities?　　　　1 2 3 4

8 How much training is given to those who teach adults or lead groups?　　　　1 2 3 4

9 To what extent is learning encouraged through different structures?　　　　1 2 3 4

10 What is the quality and availability of resources for adults in the church (filmstrips, magazines)?　　　　1 2 3 4

11 To what extent do adults in your church/group see their discipleship as a continuous process of learning, change and growth?　　　　1 2 3 4

12 How much teaching is there on the nature of the discipling process?　　　　1 2 3 4

13 How much encouragement and help is given to adults to reflect on their own experiences and to make sense of them in the light of the Christian faith?　　　　1 2 3 4

14 How much emphasis is placed on the emotional side of learning?　　　　1 2 3 4

15 To what extent are adults helped to overcome their fears of learning and change?　　　　1 2 3 4

Resources for
further study

Chapter 1

Books on discipleship in everyday life
Being Human: The nature of Spiritual Experience by Ranald Macaulay and Jerram Barrs (IVP) 1978
Spirituality and Human Emotion by Robert C Roberts (Eerdmans) 1982
Christian Behaviour by C S Lewis (Geoffrey Bles) original edition 1943
Discipleship David Watson (Hodder) 1981
Celebration of Discipline by Richard Foster (Hodder) 1980
God's people in God's world by John Gladwin (IVP) 1979
Radical Discipleship by Chris Sugden (Marshalls) 1981
Rich Christians in an age of Hunger by R J Sider (Hodder) 1977
The Call to Conversion by Jim Wallis (Lion) 1981
What is a Family? by Edith Schaeffer (Hodder Christian Paperbacks) 1975
Hidden Art by Edith Schaeffer (Norfolk Press) 1977
Three Steps Forward, Two Steps Back by C Swindoll

Books that illustrate changes in adult education
Adults as learners by K P Cross (Jossey-Bass) 1981
The Education of Adults in Britain by D Legge (Open University) 1982
Adults and Continuing Education: Theory and Practice by Peter Jarvis (Croom Helm) 1983

Books on learning in the church
Learning Community by J M Sutcliffe (Denholme House Press) 1974
Will our Children have Faith? by J H Westerhoff III (Seabury Press) 1976
Collage – information bulletin of the Christian Association for Adult and Continuing Education
What Prevents Christian Adults from Learning? by John M Hull (SCM Press) 1985

Chapter 3

Books on the learning process
Learning How to learn by Robert M Smith (Open University) 1983
Concept Formation by N Bolton (Pergamon) 1977
Learning through experiences by M Williams (Grove Pastoral Series No. 8) 1981
Adult Learning and Education by M Tight (Croom Helm) 1983
Adults: Psychological and Educational Perspectives – a series of papers published by University of Nottingham Dept. of Adult Education
Learning about Learners – especially the reader. Part of the Open University video teaching pack for Adult Educators. Also *Learning about Learning.*
Adult Learning by R Bernard Lovell (Croom Helm) 1980
Reflection: Turning Experience into Learning eds. D Boud, R Keogh, D Walker (Kogan Page) 1985

Books on adulthood
Experience of Adulthood by Leslie Francis (Gower) 1982
Some Models of Adult Learning and Adult Change by A M Huberman (Council of Europe, Strasbourg) 1974
Passages by Gail Shechy (Corgi) 1976
Adult Development and Learning by A Knox (Jossey-Bass) 1977
Facilitating Education for Older Learners by D A Peterson (Jossey-Bass) 1983

Chapter 4

Books that focus on problems in adult development/learning
Why am I afraid to love? by J Powell (Fontana) 1967
Why am I afraid to tell you who I am? by J Powell (Fontana) 1969
Together: Communicating interpersonally by Stewart and D'Angelo (Addison-Wesley) 1980
Future Shock by Alvin Toffler (Pan) 1970
Adults as learners by K P Cross (Jossey-Bass) 1981
Passages by Gail Shechy (Corgi) 1976
Born to Win by James & Jongeward (Addison-Wesley) 1971
I'm OK You're OK by Harris (Harper & Row)
The Christian at Play by Robert Johnston (Eerdmans) 1983

Chapter 5

Using Audio-visual aids
Using the Bible with Audio-visual-aids by D L Griggs (Bible Society) 1973
Seeing and Perceiving: Films in a world of Change by N Taylor and R Richardson (Ikon Publications) 1979
Know How to Use Video by David Lazell (Scripture Union) 1984

Using Overhead projectors
The Overhead Projector by Judith Wilkinson (British Council) 1979

Open Discussion
Group Discussion by Phillips, Pederson and Wood (Houghton Mifflin) 1979
Building Small Groups in the Christian Community by J Mallison (Scripture Union) 1978
Using the Bible in Groups by R Hestenes (Bible Society) 1983

Ice-breakers
Gamesters Handbook by Brandes and Phillips (Hutchinson) 1977
Gamesters 2 by D Brandes (Access Publishing, Leeds) 1982 (see also under Experiential exercises)
Communication Games by K Kruper (Free Press) 1973

Role-play
Role Play by E Milroy (Aberdeen University Press) 1982
The Effective Use of Role Play by Morry van Ments (Kogan Page) 1983

Values clarification
Values Clarification by S Simon, L Howe, H Kirschenbaum (Hart Publishing, N.Y.) 1972
Values and Faith by R Larson & D Larson (Winston Press) 1976
A Practical Guide to Value Clarification by Maury Smith (University Associates) 1977

Show and tell
Illuminative Incident Analysis by D Cortazzi & S Roole (McGraw Hill) 1975

Simulation exercises
The Trading Game (Christian Aid) – a game about Third World development
Games and Simulations in Action by A Davison and P Gordon (Woburn Press) 1978
Using Simulation Games by P Baker and M Ruth Marshall (Joint Board of Christian Education of Australia and New Zealand) 1973
More Simulation Games by P Baker and M Ruth Marshall (Joint Board as above) 1977

Making your own games
A Handbook of Game Design by H Ellington and E Addinall (Kogan Page) 1982
Simulation A Handbook for Teachers by Ken Jones (Kogan Page) 1980

Experiential exercises
Annual Handbooks for Group Facilitators by Pfeiffer and Jones (University Associates)
Handbooks (9 volumes) of Structure Experiences by Pfeiffer and Jones (University Associates)

Environment
Homegrown Christian Education by David Perry (Seabury Press) 1979 (Chapter 4)

Chapter 6

Books on preaching and lecturing
Lecturing and Explaining by G Brown (Methuen) 1978
The Recovery of Preaching by H Mitchell (Hodder & Stoughton) 1977

Books on the use of small groups
Small Groups in the Christian Community by J Mallison (SU) 1978
Creative Ideas for Small Groups in the Christian Community by J Mallison (SU) 1978
Using the Bible with Small Groups by R Hestenes (Bible Society) 1983
The Church in the Home by David Prior (Marshalls) 1983

Learning intergenerationally

Using the Bible in Teaching by D L Griggs (Bible Society) 1980

Using the Bible with all ages together by D L and P R Griggs (Bible Society) 1983

Know How: all age activities for learning and worship by M Lush (SU) 1983

Know how to encourage family worship by Howard Mellor (SU) 1984

Intergenerational activities for the church (Scripture Union Training Unit)

Homegrown Christian Education by David Perry (Seabury Press) (Chapter 5) 1979

Books on pastoral care/shepherding

Healing the Hurt Mind by David Enoch (Hodder) 1983

Soulfriend by Kenneth Leech (SPCK)

Still Small Voice by M Jacobs (SPCK) 1982

The Wisdom to Listen by M Mitton (Grove Pastoral Series No. 5) 1981

Restoring the Image by R Hurding (Paternoster) 1980

Approaches to Spiritual Direction by Anne Long (Grove Spirituality Series No. 9) 1984

Chapter 7

Training teachers of adults

Learning by Doing by W Gray & B Gerrard (Addison-Wesley) 1977

Using the Bible for all who Teach by D L Griggs (Bible Society) 1981

Freedom to Learn by Carl Rodgers (Charles E Merrill) 1983 ed

Leading small groups

Learning to Help by P Priestley and J McGuire (Tavistock Pubs) 1983

Joining Together by Johnson and Johnson (Prentice Hall) 1982 ed

Developing counselling skills

Biblical perspective on Counselling by R Inwood (Grove Pastoral Series No 11) 1980

Counselling: A skills approach by E A Munro, R J Monthen, J J Small (Methuen) 1983 ed

The Skilled Helper by G Egan (Brooks/Cole) 1975

Practical Counselling Skills by R Nelson-Jones (Holt, Reinhart & Winston) 1983

Using the Bible

Knowing God's Word by R C Sproul (SU) 1980

From Word to Life by P Yoder (Herald Press) 1980

How to Read the Bible for all its Worth by Gordon Fee & Douglas Stuart (SU) 1983

Understanding non-verbal behaviour

Non-verbal Communication in Human Interaction by M L Knapp (Holt, Rienhart & Winston) 1972

Bodily Communication by M Argyle (University Press) 1975

Personal awareness
Reaching Out by D Johnson (Prentice Hall) 1972
Interpersonal Living by G Egan (Brookes Cole) 1976

Chapter 8

Details of church book agency schemes from:
Publishers Association, 19 Bedford Square, London WC1B 3HJ
Scripture Union Bookshops, 130 City Road, London EC1V 2NJ

Magazines for bookstall managers:
Christian Update (bi-monthly), Willard Thompson Ltd., Grafton Place, Worthing, West Sussex, BN11 1QX.
The Christian Bookseller (bi-monthly), address as for above.
Denominational newspapers

Films/soundstrips/slides/videos/audio cassettes:
Scripture Union, 130 City Road, London EC1V 2NJ.
Lion Publishing, Icknield Way, Tring, Herts., HP23 4LE.
Bible Society, Stonehill Green, Westlea Down, Swindon, Wilts., SN5 7DG.
Concordia Filmstrips, 18 Cranes Way, Borehamwood, Herts., WD6 2EU.
Church Army Communication Unit, Winchester House, Independents Road, Blackheath, London SE3 9LF.
Concord Films Council Ltd., 201 Felixstowe Road, Ipswich, Suffolk, IP3 9BJ.
Church Pastoral Aid Society, Falcon Court, 32 Fleet Street, London, EC4Y 1DB.

Chapter 9

Homegrown Christian Education by David Perry (Seabury Press) 1979
Equipping God's People: Present & Future Parish Training Schemes by Peter Lewe (Grove Booklet on Ministry and Worship No 45) 1976
Helping Others Learn by P A McLagan (Addison-Wesley) 1978
Open House – Teaching and Training Material for House Groups (Church Pastoral Aid Society)
Learning all together – for all ages with special material for adults (Scripture Union)
Partners in Learning – for all ages (National Christian Education Council)
Experiments in Growth by B Caprio (Ave Maria Press) 1976
The Living Church Project by Wim Saris (Collins)
His Spirit is with us by Leslie Francis (Collins) 1981